THE FRENCH RIVIERA

BY
LINDSAY BENNETT

Produced by
Thomas Cook Publishing

Written by Lindsay Bennett

Original photography by Pete Bennett
Original design by Laburnum Technologies
Pvt Ltd

Editing and page layout by Cambridge
Publishing Management Limited,
149B Histon Road, Cambridge CB4 3JD

Published by Thomas Cook Publishing
A division of Thomas Cook Tour Operations Limited

PO Box 227, The Thomas Cook Business Park, Unit 15/16,
Coningsby Road, Peterborough PE3 8SB, United Kingdom
E-mail: books@thomascook.com
www.thomascookpublishing.com

ISBN: 1-841573-85-X

Head of Thomas Cook Publishing: Donald Greig
Project Editor: Charlotte Christensen
Project Administration: Michelle Warrington
DTP: Steven Collins

Printed and bound in Spain by: Grafo Industrias Gráficas, Basauri

Cover: Boats in harbour with town of Menton in background
Photograph by Robert Harding Picture Library Ltd/Alamy
Inside cover: All photos by Brand X Pictures/Alamy, except bottom left by
ImageGap/Alamy

CD manufacturing services provided by business interactive ltd, Rutland, UK.
CD edited and designed by Laburnum Technologies Pvt Ltd

Contents

Introduction

The name 'French Riviera' conjures up a number of vivid images, and none of them negative! 'Beautiful people' chinking champagne glasses, big wins at the gaming table at the Monte-Carlo casino, floating gin-palaces in the marinas, sizzling bodies toasting on the beach. This destination, perhaps more than any other in the world, has a reputation for 21st-century glitz and glamour.

But the Riviera is not just the hedonistic indulgence that these images suggest. A trip here can be a richly diverse experience, a *mélange* of history, culture, lifestyle, relaxation and activity that should satisfy widely different families or groups.

Pastel façades abound along the coast

The Riviera has had an enduring reputation sown with the very first seeds of the industry we call tourism. In fact, apart from 'toasting on the beach', visitors of 100 years ago would probably have roughly agreed with our initial list of 'what springs to mind' when you think 'French Riviera'. For moneyed Victorians and Edwardians, the 'grand tour' was the thing and the new *belle-époque* resorts of Cannes, Nice and Beaulieu-sur-Mer were the height of modern luxury.

Those first tourists came for the clean air, and so have generations of artists – the kind of air that allows light to reflect on azure water, the deep hue of wild lavender, the terracotta rocks of the Esterel, the jade and emerald of pines or the shimmering silver-green of olive groves – the magical colours of the south. The Riviera has a rich artistic legacy and a vibrant art community. In the 20th century, the crème de la crème called it home, following in the footsteps of 15th- to 18th-century artists, whose work graces churches across the region.

Modern artists gravitate towards the many medieval villages scattered across the hinterland. Perched on precipitous rocky outcrops or nestled deep in shady valleys, they invite exploration with their narrow cobbled alleyways, tiny squares and stone houses, whose old stables and cellars have now been transformed into chic galleries.

Tired of tramping the dusty streets? Then get active! From climbing to hiking, water skiing to windsurfing, you will find something to challenge the body. You can take to the land on horseback or mountain bike, to the water by canoe or jet-ski, or to the air under a parapente (see p160).

Or simply find yourself a pretty restaurant and sink into the almost sensual pleasure of a long French lunch, followed by an afternoon siesta to prepare for an evening open-air concert of chamber or jazz music with the heady smell of jasmine filling the air.

There are hundreds of trails to follow, hundreds of themes to choose, as you begin your own explorations. Leaflets produced by the tourist offices – on Baroque churches, haute cuisine restaurants, wine trails, in the footsteps of Picasso, the route de Napoléon, perched villages, even an underwater nature trail – will each lead you to a small corner of the landscape or a single moment in time that together make up the whole 'French Riviera'.

The brilliant hue of the water gives the Riviera its other name, the Côte d'Azur

The Place

Variety is the spice of life, so the saying goes, and nature has worked its infinite magic along the Riviera with a variety of geology, vegetation and landscape – not to mention lifestyle – seldom seen in such a small area. The 'Seeing' section has been divided into ten discrete chapters, some with obvious geographical or geological boundaries, others encompassing widely scattered attractions.

Ornate fountains were once the sole source of drinking water

Where is the Riviera?

Some call it the Riviera, others the Côte d'Azur (Azure Coast), but the boundaries of this region, which does not exist on paper, are rather flexible. To the likes of American entrepreneur Gordon Bennett, who practically invented the resort of Beaulieu-sur-Mer at the end of the 19th century, the Riviera was that short stretch of coastline between Nice and the Italian border, where he could race his sports cars along the *grande corniche*.

Later the term was extended westwards to take in Cannes and, in the 1950s, St Tropez. Today it is usual to refer to the coastal strips of two French *départements* – Alpes Maritime (06), with Nice as its regional capital, and Var (83), controlled by Toulon – but this book also adds the very eastern tip of Bouches-du-Rhône (13), using the natural boundary of the limestone *calanques* to the west of Cassis as the western limit.

Why here?

When tourists first came flocking in the mid-19th century, they stayed for months, not weeks; and they arrived in winter, not summer. Doctors were prescribing coastal air as a cure for the ills of the modern world – ills such as tuberculosis and other respiratory diseases, plus a range of 'nervous' conditions. Of course only the rich could afford it, so it soon became fashionable amongst the monied classes to leave cold, damp England, or freezing Russia, for the mild microclimate of the Riviera.

Microclimate

This microclimate has stood the Riviera in good stead for centuries. Protected by the high ground to the north, this narrow coastland for the most part misses out on frosts and high winds in winter, but cooling sea breezes temper the heat of the sun in summer, perfect for the Greeks to grow their olives and the Romans their vines, for Victorians to take strolls on the seafront in December and for modern tourists to get a tan without stewing in summer.

That is not to say that the weather smiles 365 days a year: the tourist office statistic states 300 sunny days, but rain

The attraction of the Riviera is as much about the water as it is about the land

(certainly in autumn and early spring) and the sometimes biting *mistral* winds also play a part in Riviera life.

The landscape

Where the Riviera sometimes surprises is in its great diversity. The land rises from sea level to 3,143m (10,310ft), with 80 per cent classed as mountainous. Although famed for its coast, the region has 4,000 peaks over 2,000m (6,560ft), with settlements such as St Martin-Vésubie at over 1,000m (3,280ft) above sea level offering quite a different climate and architecture to resorts and fishing communities by the sea.

The coast

The area has over 200km (125 miles) of coastline, with something to offer everyone. The Mediterranean is not a tidal sea, with no huge changes in the shape of the coastline over the course of each day, but from east to west there is infinite variety.

For sun worshippers, strands range from pebbles to fine golden sand, from wide bays such as Nice or St Tropez, where you can be sociable, to tiny coves built for two. If bathing is not your thing, try fishing from rocks or walking along coastal paths atop the cliffs, gasping at the vertiginous drops. Then

Take time out to relax between museums

do not forget the natural harbours, such as Villafranche-sur-Mer or Toulon, where fishing boats still hang on to a dying industry while pleasure boats cater to the ever-increasing number of tourists. The Giens peninsula is perhaps the most unusual feature – not one, but two sand spits now link this tiny island to the coast.

The rocks

The rock sub-strata which comprise the Riviera are complicated. The interior, in the Var to the west, is a limestone layer which rises to mountain chains near Toulon. It has thin soil and monumental underground cave systems carved out over aeons, best seen at La Baume Obscure.

The Maures mountains, west of St Tropez, are old and crystalline; their neighbours to the east, the Esterel, are older still, comprising red porphyry or volcanic rock now eroded into columns or jagged narrow *calanques* or inlets. The Maritime Alps – their snow-capped peaks can be seen in the distance to the north – are crowned by the Massif du Mercantour, from which the national park of the region takes its name.

The rivers

Rivers capture the paradox of the Riviera. Almost dry in summer, when tourists laugh at the folly of building an expensive bridge over a trickle, they spring to life in winter and spring – sometimes flooding with disastrous results when there is a deluge in the hinterland.

The numerous gorges that carve their way across the landscape – the Verdon and Vésubie are the most impressive – display the power of the seasonal flow that characterises the area.

Vegetation

Throughout the Riviera, humans have altered the landscape but particularly the vegetation, taking over much of the cultivable land for olives, vines and other fruits, such as lemons, and flowers. However, almost half of France's 4,200 floral species grow here, with over 40 species endemic to the area. Alpes-Maritimes *département* is the only place in Europe that possesses every level of vegetation from Mediterranean, at sea-level, to Alpine, in the mountains.

Native forests are the natural cover in the lowlands, mostly scrub oak and pine interspersed with plane and cypress. Almond and chestnut also thrive, and both are cash crops for the locals. At ground level the limestone areas are blanketed by *garrigue* – thorns (gorse and thistle) mixed with lavender and aromatic herbs (thyme and rosemary) – whilst the sandy soils support a more succulent green brushwood called *maquis*.

Forest fires are a constant threat in the hills behind the coast

History

c. **6000** BC	Oldest remains of human activity so far found along the Riviera, at the Grotte de Vallonet near Roquebrune-Cap-Martin.
c. **1800– 1500** BC	Early Bronze Age man carves images on the rocks at the Vallée des Merveilles.
c. **1000** BC	Ligurian peoples settle around the Marseille basin and along the coast.
600 BC	Marseille is founded by Greek settlers.
500–400 BC	The Greeks expand to colonise Antibes, Hyères, Nice, Monaco and St Tropez.
c. **58** BC	The Romans take Gaul (roughly, modern France).
49 BC	Julius Caesar founds Fréjus; Romans develop existing Greek settlements.
c. **5** BC	Trophée des Alpes erected to commemorate Roman victories.
1st–3rd centuries AD	Roman settlements develop along the Via Aurelia, the Roman road along the Riviera coast.

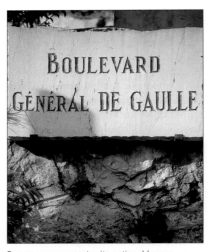

France commemorates its national heroes

313	Edict of Milan grants religious freedom. Early Christian communities founded; some develop into bishoprics.
4th–5th centuries	With the fall of Rome, northern tribes such as the Vandals and Goths invade or sack the Riviera.
8th–9th centuries	Saracens invade from the sea, settling in many coastal areas.
800	Charlemagne rules much of what is now France.
843	Charlemagne's land is divided between his sons: Lothair is given Provence, including much of the Riviera.

10th–12th centuries	The counts of Provence rule the area with relative independence, supported by other feudal lords. Later the counts become vassals of Toulouse, then Barcelona.
1246	Charles of Anjou becomes Count of Provence.
1308	Monaco is bought by the Grimaldi family.
1343	Jeanne becomes Queen of Provence.
13th–14th centuries	Black Death depletes the region: half the population may have perished.
1388	Nice cedes itself to the counts of Savoy, breaking with the counts of Provence.
1434	'Good' King René becomes Count of Provence.
1481	Charles of Maine (then Count of Provence) cedes his lands to Louis XI, King of France. Provence (not including Nice) officially becomes part of France in 1486.
1524	Provence is invaded by the Bourbons, rivals for the French throne.
	Monaco is occupied by Spain and given the title 'principality'.
1536	Charles V invades Provence.
1539	The Provençal language is suppressed after French is made the official language.
1543	Nice is attacked by French troops, supported by Ottoman forces.
1550–98	Wars of Religion in France.
1598	Edict of Nantes grants religious freedom for all citizens.
1641	The Spanish leave Monaco, but it is immediately taken by the French.

The Romans built some fine towns along the Riviera

1691	Nice is taken by the French, but returned to Savoy in 1696.
1707	Savoyard forces invade southern Provence, along the Riviera.
1718	County of Nice becomes part of the Kingdom of Sardinia.
1720	Another great plague decimates the area.
1789	The French Revolution.
1790	The old counties are abolished and Provence is broken into three *départements* – Bouches-du-Rhône, Var and Basses-Alpes.
1793	Siege of Toulon by the British. Nice is ceded to France.
1804	Napoléon Bonaparte becomes Emperor.
1814	Napoléon abdicates and departs from St-Raphaël to exile on Elba. The French leave Monaco, and Nice is taken back by Sardinia.
1815	Napoléon breaks out from exile, landing at Golfe-Juan before heading north. Later, the

	Battle of Waterloo finishes Napoléon's career. Sardinia takes Monaco.
c. **1830**	English aristocrats visit to take the mild winter air around Nice.
1861	Nice is finally ceded to France for good under the Treaty of Nice. Monaco frees itself from Sardinian control and Emperor Napoléon III buys Menton and Roquebrune from the principality. One thousand families now take winter holidays in the region.

Picturesque narrow alleyways were originally designed for defence

1863	The first Casino opened in Monte-Carlo, to boost revenue for the principality.
1892	The artist Paul Signac lands at St Tropez, kick-starting the rise of the resort.
1907	Another artist, Auguste Renoir, settles at Cagnes-sur-Mer.
1914	The foreign colony (English, Russian and German) in the Riviera reaches 150,000; the fine Negresco and Carlton hotels are built.
1920s	The artists Signac and Modigliani 'discover' St-Paul.
1931	The first summer season begins, with one hotel opening its doors.
1944	Provence is liberated by the Americans.
1946	French women get the vote. The first Cannes film festival is held. Picasso moves to a studio in Antibes castle.
1947	The Roya valley (Tende area) becomes part of France.

Vauban designed fortifications to protect the French coastline

1956	Prince Rainier of Monaco marries the Hollywood star, Grace Kelly.
1973	Death of Picasso.
1980	The A8 *autoroute* is built. Monaco develops Fontvielle, reclaiming land from the sea.
1982	Death of Princess Grace of Monaco.
2001	French franc replaced by the euro.
2003	Forest fires devastate 10,000 hectares (24,700 acres) of the Riviera. Four people die, 20,000 are evacuated.

Governance

During the 1990s, French farmers brought Paris to a halt when a convoy of tractors made its way through the city to deposit a pile of steaming manure in the gateway of the Élysée Palace, the French President's official home. It is part of the French psyche to take such direct action when the government does not seem to be listening. After all, perhaps the most famous event in French history started with people power.

'Liberty', proclaims the rights of all French people

THE LAST 200 YEARS

With the French Revolution, the common man made his feelings clear in no uncertain terms. Many of the upper classes lost their head to 'Madame Guillotine' and a new Republican world order began. *Liberté, Egalité, Fraternité* (Freedom, Equality, Brotherhood) were enshrined in the inaugural French constitution in 1792, and these concepts are still taken very seriously today, including the freedom to take direct action when people feel it necessary. Since the Revolution, the French have had a healthy respect for the political process but a deep distrust of politicians, the people who wield power on their behalf. People of every stratum of society agree that governance 'ain't what it used to be'.

The fact that Paris is the seat of government rankles a little in the south. To many, it is bad enough that they had the French language forced on them, when they spoke their own, Provençal, until the mid-16th century. In any case, a lot of the Riviera did not become French soil until quite recently (Nice in 1860, Menton and Roquebrune in 1861). Or perhaps it is a matter of hotter 'Latin' blood in the south, against the 'cooler' disposition of the northerners.

Although now in a period of stability, there have been threats to the republic, not least from Napoléon Bonaparte who took upon himself the French crown, though as emperor, not king, in 1804. Had his plans to conquer the whole of Europe been successful, the republic might have been doomed, but Napoléon's Waterloo was a victory for representative government.

Since the initial revolution there have been 16 rewritings of the constitution and five new republics. The last debacle was the Algerian War of Independence in the 1950s, which wrought political chaos and social unrest. The French government was brought to its knees by the impending loss of its greatest colony, its lack of positive action to deal with the issue and the resulting flood of migrants that swamped the south coast. The constitution collapsed in 1958, to be replaced by the one still in use today.

Many stately town halls stand testament to France's pride in the Republican constitution

THE FIFTH REPUBLIC (1958–PRESENT DAY)

Though today the French have two houses of parliament, the Assemblée Nationale (National Assembly) and the Sénat (Senate), the role of the President is much more than that of a simple figurehead. Presidential powers were written into the constitution by the incumbent, Charles de Gaulle, in reaction to the problems of 1958, though ironically he lost power in 1968 after mass student uprisings and country-wide strikes.

The president

The French president leads national policy, appoints the Prime Minister and government, and wields power in the fields of foreign affairs and defence. He can dissolve parliament and can assume dictatorial powers in a national crisis. Directly elected by the people every seven years, the president can have no more than two periods in office. Any French citizen over 23 is eligible to become president.

Parliament

Parliament plays a slightly secondary role compared to many representational bodies in Europe. The National Assembly, the lower house, has 577 directly elected députés (deputies); elections take place every five years. The Senate is an indirectly elected body of

318 chosen by some 130,000 local councillors (usually from amongst themselves). They have a nine-year mandate, with one third being replaced every three years.

The voting system

In most elections, France operates a modified first-past-the-post system. To win, candidates must get over half the votes; otherwise a second ballot a week later chooses between the top two candidates.

Political parties

The main political parties in France are the Rassemblement pour la République (PRP), the conservative party founded by General de Gaulle and also known as Gaullists; the Union pour la Démocratie Française (UDF), the Democratic centrist party, incorporating the Parti Républicain founded by ex-president Giscaird d'Estaing; the Parti Socialiste and the Parti Communiste – both left wing; and the Front National, the right-wing nationalist party.

It has been known for parties to form alliances to beat their rivals and the French are known for their tactical voting – that is, voting for one party so that another does not get elected, rather than voting for their own first choice.

Local government

There is a strong history of local government within France. The country is divided into 22 regions, which are

Bleu–blanc–rouge: the French flag flies outside all official buildings

made up of 95 *départements*. The Riviera, part of the Provence–Alpes–Côte d'Azur region, cuts across the *départements* of Alpes-Maritime, Var and just into the Bouches-du-Rhône, and contains over 3,000 cantons and 36,000 communes.

Communes

Communes are the smallest political unit, but range in size from large cities to small villages. Communes are controlled by a *maire* (mayor), elected every six years, who has wide-ranging powers as head of the municipal council and local representative of the state – a role that evokes an immense pride and

The press plays an important part in political debate

sense of responsibility. The role of mayor is seen as the launching pad for a greater political career – President Jacques Chirac rose to prominence as mayor of Paris. Most deputies and senators in the parliament chambers are mayors of their local communes.

The legal system

Notoriously bureaucratic, but it works, the system is based on written civil law as laid down by Napoléon in 1789. Called the *code Napoléon* (Napoleonic Law), it covers all aspects of civil, fiscal and penal law. Unlike the British and US systems, for example, there are no 'juries of your peers' or 'twelve good men and true'; cases are heard by a tribunal of professional and lay judges, where a two-thirds majority results in a guilty verdict.

THE FRENCH AND EUROPE

One of the founding fathers and most vocal supporters of European co-operation, France may seem unequivocally pro-Brussels, but in reality the country still dances to its own tune. Farmers grow increasingly concerned about the seemingly doomed Common Agricultural Policy – France's baby from the start, as it had a huge agricultural sector to protect – and small producers lament European standardisation laws, which have meant the disappearance of many traditional foods. France's decision in 2003–4 to ignore EU/euro financial rules, and take their budgets into deficit, is the most recent signal that the 'Marseillaise' is not going to be replaced by some bland pan-European anthem – yet.

Culture

The French have long feted their own literati, having produced some of the world's most renowned thinkers, artists and writers. They have also appreciated the good taste of foreign cultural figures who have lived and worked in France. The seeds of many of the finest flowers of philosophy, art and drama were planted here, and France still stands at the forefront of cultural growth, especially in the francophone world.

Modern architecture is a feature of the region

Art

France has been a leader in the world of art, especially since the mid-18th century. A list of French artists reads like a 'who's who' of painters, with names like Signac, Seurat, Renoir, Toulouse-Lautrec, Monet, Gauguin, Matisse and Chagall.

This strength in depth attracted foreign artists, inspired by the French landscape and lifestyle, most famously, Picasso.

Artists have been particularly drawn to the Riviera, because of its light, its landscapes and its lifestyles, and settled in the area – Renoir in Cagnes-sur-Mer, Signac in St Tropez, and Picasso in Antibes, Vallauris and Mougins.

This tradition continues: in the 1960s Nouvelle Réalisme was born in Nice, led by Klein and César, who pushed Pop Art in new directions and spawned the famed Nice School. Their work can be seen in the Musée d'Art Moderne et d'Art Contemporain in the city.

Architecture

The Riviera is rich in architecture, from the Roman era to the present day, but for many generations its architecture has been more practical than aesthetic.

The wonderful small villages perched on hilltops – that area hallmark of the region – came about for defence. The fortified châteaux at their heart protected the whole village if need be, whilst their narrow winding alleyways and small windows were meant to baffle the enemy rather than add charm and character.

Religious architecture is also a key feature, from simple Romanesque chapels to the Gothic cathedrals of the early and late Middle Ages. Gothic (of which there is a wealth in the Roya valley) gave way to neo-Gothic and neo-Romanesque, and the Riviera even has several fine Russian Orthodox churches, plus 20th-century decoration by Cocteau, Matisse and Chagall.

The *belle époque* was a high point of architectural excellence for the region, coinciding with the arrival of mass tourism. The first flood of money resulted in the building of the great hotels: the Negresco, Westminster and

Excelsior in Nice, the Hôtel de Paris and Hermitage in Monte-Carlo, and the Carlton in Cannes. Some entrepreneurs went further, building their own private 'palaces' such as the Riviera at Beaulieu and the Villa Ephrussi at St-Jean-Cap-Ferrat.

This highly developed eye for aesthetics combines with the economic buoyancy of the Riviera to ensure it is one of the most vibrant areas in Europe for modern architectural projects. Nice Côte d'Azur Airport has won several awards whilst the Musée d'Art Moderne et d'Art Contemporain (1990) kick-started a redevelopment of several city blocks, including the Bibliothèque Municipale de Louis-Nucéra, a giant box (the human head) supported by a column designed to look like a neck.

Music

Though France has not so great a history of musical composition, every year there are thousands of live music performances on the Riviera – Baroque, choral, opera, jazz – and a number of renowned festivals.

The Riviera's permanent companies include the Orchestre Philharmonique de Monte-Carlo (*www.opmc.mc*), Orchestre Philharmonique and Choeur Philharmonique (*www.nice-cotedazur.org*), Opéra de Nice and Opéra de Monte-Carlo (*www.opera.mc*).

Literature

French literature is punctuated with great names, from the medieval troubadour Chrétien de Troyes to Victor Hugo, not to mention Dumas,

Balzac and Proust, though there is no modern author quite so admired. However, the country also has a strength in intellectual and philosophical debate, including the 20th-century luminary Jean-Paul Sartre.

The light, landscape and lifestyle of the Riviera have also fostered innovative volumes from French and international authors. Simone de Beauvoir, André Breton, George Sand and Paul Valéry are amongst the best-known native authors, but add to these names like Graham Greene, Aldous Huxley, Ernest Hemingway, Thomas Mann, H G Wells, Oscar Wilde and F Scott Fitzgerald – who captures the essence of ex-patriot life on the Riviera in *Tender is the Night* (1934).

France's colonial past features in street art

Theatre

The founding of the Comédie Française (*www.comedie-francaise.fr*) in Paris in 1680 started a national love of the theatre and the capital now enjoys a wealth of stage performances. The Comédie still concentrates on the classics, and the 'bards' of French literature (Molière, Victor Hugo and others) are revisited each season, but France has also invested in modern theatre in the French language. The Centre Dramatique National Nice Côte d'Azur (in Nice) has developed a reputation as a centre of excellence for all genres but there are also over 20 other theatres along the Riviera.

Cinema

French cinema is one of the world's most vibrant, with successes of every kind, from comedy such as *M. Hulot's Holiday* to dramas like *Manon des Sources.* Do not forget that it was Louis Lumière who invented moving pictures in the 1890s. French cinematographers have always concentrated on the complexity of human relations in their

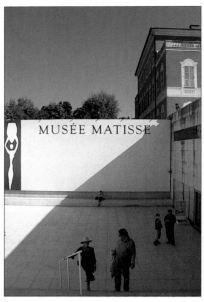

Matisse bequeathed his private collection to the city of Nice

Though Spanish, Picasso was adopted by the French and did much of his later work on the Riviera at Antibes

storylines – heavier and more intellectual than the entertainment of Hollywood.

French cinema also helps to ensure the continuing vitality of the French language and is encouraged by the Académie Française. The French government ploughs millions of euros into the industry, with directors such as Luc Besson breaking through the language barrier into world cinema.

The Riviera has long been used as a backdrop in films, from *César* (1936) – filmed in Toulon, written by the Provençal Marc Pagnol and starring Raimu, who lived in Cogolin – to *Herbie goes to Monte-Carlo* (1977). That year the famed 'Love Bug' toured the coast.

French neo-classical design at Beaulieu-sur-Mer

Haute couture

French chic is almost a cultural cliché, but step out onto any city street, especially along the Riviera, and you will feel that the French are born with an innate sense of style. Perhaps they have a unique gene, that scientists will discover 100 years from now, that allows them to look incredibly right with apparently little effort.

This must be why they were able to 'invent' *haute couture*, a process of raising clothes to an art form, led by Coco Chanel but carried on by Christian Dior, with his post-war 'new look', and Yves Saint-Laurent.

They understand completely that French desire for perfection of form that links the couturiers directly with the great artists. Today's masterpieces decorate the body!

Villa Grecque Kérylos

Festivals and Events

The Riviera's calendar could not be more full, with an average of ten events for each day of the year. The range is wide, with world-acclaimed celebrations of sporting and performing arts side by side with age-old traditional festivities and reverential religious processions.

This is really just a small selection, in date order, so check with CRT for a full list.

Cannes film festival souvenirs are on sale all year round

Candlemas Fair
2 Feb, Grimaud

Lemon Festival
Mid-Feb–mid-Mar, Menton
130 tonnes of lemons and other citrus fruit decorate floats for this carnival.

Mimosa Procession
Third Sun in Feb, Bormes-les-Mimosas

Mardi Gras
14 days before Shrove Tuesday, Nice
Dating back to 1294, Nice Carnival is one of the most spectacular in Europe: over a million spectators cheer on the processions.

Procession of the Entombment of Christ
Evening of Good Friday, Roquebrune-Cap-Martin

Provençal Folklore Festival
Easter Sunday and Monday, Vence

Monte-Carlo Tennis Masters Tournament
April, Monaco
Prelude to the European Grand Slam season.

International Film Festival
May, Cannes
Sees the *crème de la crème* competing for the coveted 'Palme d'Or' but the public are limited to star-spotting outside screening venues or glitzy parties.

F1 Monaco Grand Prix
Ascension Day weekend, Monte-Carlo
For qualifying on Sat and race on Sun, the principality is turned into a giant race-track. The best seats need to be booked well in advance.

The Bravade
17 May, St Tropez
Is a religious and historical procession.

Rose Festival
Last weekend in May, Grasse
Procession and decorated floats.

Fisherman's Votive Festival
29 June, St Tropez
A procession follows the votive statue around the town and harbour to pray for the safety of the fishermen and bless future catches.

World Jazz Festival
Mid-July, Juan-les-Pins
Since 1960 one of the premier jazz
festivals in the world, with open-air
concerts in The Gould pine grove.

Bastille Day
14 July, across France
Celebrates the storming of the Bastille
prison in Paris, which started the
Revolution. Marches and fireworks.

Jasmine Festival
First Sun in Aug, Grasse
The air is heady with scent as this
parade celebrates the year's new crop.

International Chamber Music Festival
August, Menton
Open-air performances in front of the
Basilica of St Michel.

Pottery Festival
13 August, Vallauris
Celebrates the town's most famous
export.

La Nioulargue Sailing Regatta
First weekend in Oct, St Tropez
Building autumn offshore breezes offer
serious sailors some serious competition.

Garlic Fair
6 Oct, Fréjus

National Day
19 Nov, Monaco
Parades and fireworks displays.

Shepherds' Pastorale
25 Dec, Lucéram
With guided tour of over 1,000 *crèches*
or Nativity scenes around the village.

Garlic: celebrated for its importance in southern French cuisine, garlic has its own fair in Fréjus each
October

Artistic Movements and the Riviera

You can spend many an hour in galleries filled with priceless masterpieces, so it helps to know your Dada from your Pointillism. Here is an introduction to the artistic styles you are likely to encounter on the Riviera.

Primitive

This style is seen in churches all across the area. The term generally indicates work completed before the Renaissance, which embraced classical form and revolutionised art. The best-known Primitive artist of the Riviera was Louis Bréa.

Naïve

This is painting in a straightforward style that lacks – indeed, often rejects – sophisticated artistic techniques.

Impressionist

This movement developed in France in the later 19th century, and aimed to create an impression of the moment, especially the effects of light and colour, rather than an accurate depiction. Monet (its leading exponent) visited Antibes, and Renoir settled in Cagnes-sur-Mer.

Pointillist

A neo-Impressionist technique using tiny dots of pure colour, which merge when viewed from a distance. This produces greater luminosity and brilliance of colour. From the French *pointiller* ('to mark with dots'). The movement was created by Seurat, whose disciple Paul Signac settled in St Tropez, where other artists such as Matisse gravitated.

Fauvist

A movement that began in 1905 as a reaction against Impressionism, with the use of vivid expressionism and non-naturalistic colour. It was named by art critic Louis Vauxcelles when, on entering a gallery with a Renaissance statue surrounded by these canvases, he remarked 'Donatello au milieu des fauves' ('Donatello among wild beasts'). Leading lights were Matisse and Dufy, who lived in Nice.

Cubist

A revolution against the traditional modes of representation. It abandoned perspective from a single viewpoint and used interlocking planes and geometric shapes. This movement, also named by Vauxcelles (in 1908), was created by Braque and Picasso – who in later life lived in various towns on the Riviera (Mougins, Cannes and Vallauris) – but was also taken up by Fernand Léger, who lived and worked in Biot.

Dada

Mocking artistic convention and emphasising the absurd, Dada was launched in Zurich in 1916 and given its name – meaning 'hobbyhorse' – after a review that appeared in Zurich in that year. Max Ernst was a major force and he settled in Seillans for the final years of his life.

Surrealist

Developed from Dada, Surrealism was launched in 1924 and used the creative potential of the unconscious mind by the irrational juxtaposition of images, emotive colour and dream imagery. Max Ernst developed into a Surrealist, and Russian-born Marc Chagall carried on the movement, leaving various works along the coast and in his museum in Nice.

Nouvelle Réalisme

Emerging in the 1960s in opposition to the continued popularity of abstract forms, Nouvelle Réalisme was influenced by the Pop Art movement in the USA. Its main exponent was Frenchman Yves Klein, who founded the Nice School, a major influence on world art during the 1970s.

Opposite top: A 'surreal' image of a famous post-Impressionist
Opposite bottom: A Cubist mosaic by Fernand Léger
Above: This medieval château in Antibes, where Picasso had a studio, now houses the Picasso Museum

Impressions

Before you rush headlong into the undoubted delights of the French Riviera, this section offers practical information and a little cultural background. By no means exhaustive or scientific, it is a sort of 'social snapshot' to help you build a picture of where you are going.

Lose yourself in the narrow cobbled streets

WHEN TO TRAVEL

Despite its reputation as a summer destination, over half the Riviera's visitors arrive in the other three seasons, making it an all-year-round holiday location. However, its character does change through the year, so bear in the mind the following when choosing when to come.

Summer

Average daytime temperatures sit in the mid-20s °C (75–81°F) but can and do rise to the mid-30s °C (92–98°F), so it is hot, and dry. School holidays see the

French and half of Europe arriving in their hordes. It is difficult to get around because the roads are clogged. On the plus side, all the facilities are fully open, from water sports companies, to nightclubs, to hotels and campsites.

Autumn

The high season stops abruptly when French children return to school and Paris opens up again at the end of August. The weather tempers a little but is still warm; it is easier to get a seat at your favourite restaurant and prices for hotel rooms drop a little. From mid-

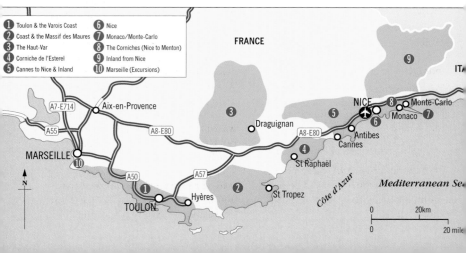

1 Toulon & the Varois Coast
2 Coast & the Massif des Maures
3 The Haut-Var
4 Corniche de l'Esterel
5 Cannes to Nice & Inland
6 Nice
7 Monaco/Monte-Carlo
8 The Corniches (Nice to Menton)
9 Inland from Nice
10 Marseille (Excursions)

FRANCE

ITA

A7-E714   Aix-en-Provence

A55

3

Draguignan

NICE
8   Monte-Carlo
5   6   Monaco   7
9

MARSEILLE
10

A8-E80

A8-E80   Antibes
Cannes

4
St Raphaël

A50   A57

1   2
Hyères   St Tropez

TOULON

Côte d'Azur

Mediterranean Se

N

0   20km
0   20 mile

French cafés are perfect places for socialising

September, water sports and other summer activities stop, and some craftsmen take a few weeks off after their busy time.

Winter

No water sports, and some Riviera resorts take on the atmosphere of retirement communities with few faces under the age of 70. Restaurants and bars have more French atmosphere, hotel rooms in all categories are easier to find and museums are delightfully uncrowded.

Spring

The days get longer and warmer once again and everything seems to be in bloom, including the flower fields of Grasse.

GETTING AROUND

The Riviera's population is concentrated in a small area and it swells hugely in high season. This puts pressure on all transport systems, but particularly on the roads. Traffic jams are commonplace, especially in the cities and along the coastal highways. Perhaps the worst time is at the end of a day on the beach, when everyone is heading home around 6pm. You will always wait in traffic to get into St Tropez and to get through Nice.

Inland, roads can be narrow and twisting, and the spectacular vistas can be distracting – drivers should take extra care.

One way to avoid road traffic is to take the train. Service along the middle section of the Riviera (between Fréjus and Nice) provides a good alternative to the car, especially if you want to explore resorts like Nice, Antibes, La Napoule or Cannes. The line also offers excellent vistas of the Corniche de l'Esterel.

GETTING STARTED
Manners and customs
Greetings

When introduced to a French person you should shake hands and say 'good day' (*Bonjour, madame* or *Bonjour, monsieur*). You should also say *Bonjour* when entering a shop, bar or restaurant, especially in the countryside. For such cases, the French have a single phrase covering mixed-sex groups: you can say '*Bonjour messieurs-dames*'.

You should also say 'goodbye' – *Au revoir* or *Bonne journée* ('have a good day') – when leaving shops and bars. *Other useful phrases:*

Bon soir ('good evening') is a greeting to be used from about 6pm for the rest of the evening.

Bonne soirée – means 'have a good evening' – use it when you leave a group or individual and some of the evening remains.

Bonne nuit – 'goodnight' – is to be used at the end of the evening.

Titles (*monsieur* or *madame*) should be used when addressing mature people.

The correct response to *merci* ('thank you') is *je vous en prie*, roughly meaning 'you're welcome'.

To kiss or not to kiss

This kiss (*bise*) is not a kiss on the mouth, nor in reality a kiss on the cheek: it is almost a coming-together of cheeks whilst the mouth makes a kissing motion. It is a greeting amongst people who know each other, so it will not be an issue on first meeting. On the second meeting, take your cue from your French friends – women will offer their cheeks while men will lean toward you.

Women kiss women and men in the group, whilst men kiss women but shake hands with men. The number of kisses varies according to place, from one to four (four being the norm in the Riviera, two on each side). Children will expect to be kissed.

Services between Fréjus and Nice: no traffic jams

Familiar or formal

When addressing people (English 'you'), the French language has two forms. The word *vous* when addressing people is a plural (more than one person) but it is also the formal address, used when speaking to people you have not met before or do not know well, or in official situations. Also, it is not normal in French society to call people by their first names if you have only just met.

The use of the less formal or intimate *tu* happens at the instigation of the French, as does the use of a person's first name. Rules are different for children, who should always be addressed as *tu* or by name. Younger people (under 30) are much less formal, but you should

Poised for *la bise* – a normal greeting between friends

not address older persons by their first name unless invited to do so – address them as *monsieur* or *madame*.

Good manners

Always wish the people at your table *bon appétit* ('good appetite') before starting a meal. This will be equally appreciated if you pass people at an alfresco table or having a picnic.

See and be seen on the Riviera

The toast before taking a drink is *santé* ('health').

Siesta?

Although city folks do not always take a siesta, once you start exploring villages in the hinterland you will find a three-hour afternoon break is the norm. If you still insist on touring the little villages at this time, try not to make too much noise, but – even better – relax over a long lunch rather than braving the midday heat.

Culture shock?

The French are a complicated people and many Francophiles will admit that, no matter how often they visit the country, the people have the constant ability to delight, surprise and frustrate in equal measure. After all, this is the country that gave the world hot-air ballooning, the bikini, Jean-Paul Gaultier and the metric system.

'Franglais'

The French have been fighting the spread of the English language for decades, but have made a concerted effort since American language and culture began its march across the globe. The French government introduced rules such as 'only so many foreign-language tracks to be played on radio each hour', or 'all foreign films to be dubbed into French' but to no avail. French youth has been seduced by '*le weekend*' and MacDonalds to the chagrin of intellectuals and conservatives, and the whole issue really became a moot point with the arrival of Disneyland Paris in the 1990s.

Ignoring trivial rules

The French love of bureaucracy is legendary, but so is their ability to ignore rules if it suits them. Thus, locals park anywhere they please, smoke in no-smoking areas and exercise their canine pals where it says 'no dogs allowed'.

Smoking

Smoking is not considered a bad habit in France; it is a national pastime that is regarded as cool, especially by the young. You will not be able to avoid smoke in restaurants and bars, even if you sit at a no-smoking table (which bars and restaurants are by law supposed to set aside). Asking a Frenchman to desist will simply incur a Gallic shrug at best, and outright abuse at worst. Luckily the mild climate allows non-smokers to sit outside on the terrace for a meal or drink for much of the year.

Lap dogs

Though the French are not known as animal lovers, there is one creature that has a firm place in their hearts: the lap dog.

These pampered pooches are more accessory than pet, sporting ribbons or coats to match their owners. Toileted and preened they never need to use their legs, being carried under the arm or in a chi-chi bag. They accompany their owners everywhere, even having their own seats in restaurants, and receive regular kisses in the same fashion as small children.

Dog dirt

The downside of thousands of lap dogs is the amount of dog dirt on the streets.

In most large towns, streets and pavements are washed down daily and it is the responsibility of shop keepers and householders to keep the area outside their property clean. However, watch your step down alleyways and always when walking across parkland.

Social *faux pas*

Although you will be able to wear almost nothing on the beach without a problem, it is not acceptable to wander around towns in beachwear, unless it can pass as ultra-fashionable town wear. Bare chests for men are a definite no-no once you leave the strand!

When is a drink not a drink?

Cafés in the coastal resorts are not about drinking to satisfy a thirst – these are the places to sit in your most fashionable garb to 'see and be seen'. You will need to invest in a good pair of sunglasses so that you can watch the world go by, while still looking the epitome of cool.

A FRENCH RIVIERA MUSEUMS PASS

The regional tourist organisation issues a pass, which is valid for selected monuments, museums and gardens in the region (though not all attractions subscribe to the scheme, so ask before buying). The passes are valid for a number of consecutive days from 1 to 25 and represent a good cost saving on individual entry fees if your itinerary is attraction-heavy. They are available from main tourist offices and FNAC shops. (FNAC is a chain of French stores selling magazines, books and CDs.)

Toulon and the Varois Coast

The westernmost part of the Riviera, the Varois coast is the region's wine-making district, its hillsides blanketed in vines. The coastline has great variety, from sandy bays to limestone crags, while inland its ranges of low hills shelter medieval villages and offer panoramic views over the sea. Anchoring the territory is the bustling city of Toulon, a major naval port since the 16th century.

Fresh fish, a staple of Mediterranean cuisine

Bandol

Entre mer et vignes ('between the sea and the vines') is the slogan of this coastal resort, which gives its name to one of the most renowned wines of the Riviera. On the rolling hills around the town are several vineyards offering *dégustation* ('tasting') of their most recently bottled wines. Discovered in the 19th century by the first generation of 'tourists', including authors Aldous Huxley and Thomas Mann, the large port now devoted to pleasure craft was once busy with wine shipping. The port promenade, allée Jean-Moulin, is a focal point for strollers by day and evening.

Some 3km (2 miles) north of the town, the Jardin Exotique et Zoo de Sanary-Bandol (Tropical Garden and Zoo) displays exceptional tropical plants and cacti, along with animals from capuchin monkeys to peccaries.

Seven-minute boat trips from the port take you to the tiny Île de Bendor. Owned by the estate of industrialist Paul Ricard, the island hosts Espace Paul-Ricard, with workshops for aspiring artists, and Exposition Universelle des Vins (World of Wine Exhibition) which displays over 8,000 bottles of wine from around the world.

Jardin Exotique et Zoo de Sanary-Bandol. Tel: 04 94 29 40 38. Open: Mon–Sat 8am–12pm, 2–6pm, Sun and public holidays 2–6pm, except June–Sept 2–7pm. Admission fee.

Espace Paul-Ricard & Exposition Universelle des Vins, Ile de Bendor, 83150 Bandol. Tel: 04 94 29 44 34. Open: 10am–12pm, 2–6pm. Closed: Wed and Oct–Easter. Free.

Les Calanques Massif

Lying between Marseille and Cassis, the *calanques* (creeks) form a dramatic natural western boundary to the Riviera. These deep, fjord-like inlets cut into jagged white limestone cliffs, resulting in one of the most spectacular coastlines in France – the reflections of rock through the shallow water are innumerable shades of blue and green.

This stone, quarried for centuries, has been used in the port at Marseille and at Alexandria in Egypt. The rocks also hold vast quantities of fresh water in caves and crevices, a valuable resource for local people over the centuries.

The *calanques* make a popular boat trip from Cassis. Port Miou Calanque is a winding, narrow inlet lined with small boats, while Port Pin is the smallest and En Vau the most stunning, with a tiny golden beach at its mouth. They are popular with climbers who like serrated limestone peaks and hikers who reach them along the cliff-top footpaths.

Cap Sicié

This cape, at the western mouth of the rade de Toulon (Toulon harbour),

rises 298m (980ft) almost vertically out of the sea. Atop the peak is the church of Notre Dame du Mai (Our Lady of the May Tree) containing votive offerings, from sailors wishing divine protection out at sea and from those with injuries or illness. It has excellent views across the harbour, with the Toulon mountains in the background, and numerous footpaths through the woodland.

Cassis

Though technically not in the Riviera (it lies just over the Var border in

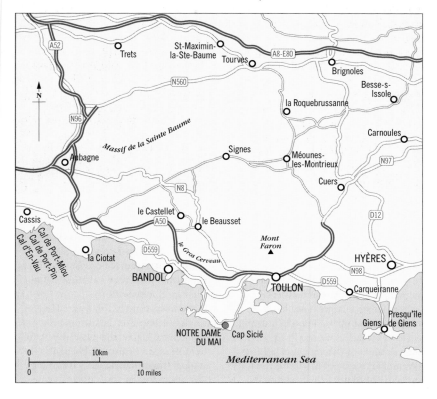

Dramatic coastal views at Cap Sicié

Bouches-du-Rhône), it would really be a shame to miss Cassis.

Pastel cottages cascading down to a tiny port flanked by cliffs, it has all the ingredients of a classic Mediterranean fishing village – there is still a fish market on the quayside each morning. Also on the quayside, the Prud'hommie des pêcheurs or fishing court holds a ceremonial statue of St Pierre which is carried aloft during the traditional festival (*last weekend in June*). The Musée Arts et Traditions Populaires (Museum of Art and Popular Traditions) has further displays on the festival and other local traditions.

The town church, consecrated in 1867, is a fine example in Cassis stone (*see Les Calanques p32*) but the most impressive building is the 14th-century citadel (the original Cassis) overlooking the town, which is now someone's dream home.

The landscape around Cassis was the inspiration for French poet Frédéric Mistral's *Calandel*, his seminal work. Mistral also coined the famous phrase *Qu'a vist Paris … Se noun a vist Cassis, pou dire: n'ai rèn vist* ('He who has seen Paris, but not Cassis, hasn't seen anything').
Musée Arts et Traditions Populaires, Maison de Cassis, rue Xavier d'Authier, 13260 Cassis. Tel: 04 42 01 88 66. Open: Wed, Thur, Sat in summer, 3.30–6.30pm; winter, 2.30–5.30pm. Admission fee.

Pretty town square on Presqu'île de Giens

Le Castellet

Perched on a hillside surrounded by the vineyards of the Bandol region, le Castellet is a medieval village stronghold build around the 11th-century citadel. Within the well-preserved ramparts around the austere Romanesque church (l'Église de la Transfiguration) and the château (now the town hall) are 17th- and 18th-century buildings, housing arts shops and restaurants with local wines on their menus.

Hyères

This southernmost mainland Riviera resort is also one of the oldest established, having developed during the 18th century. Queen Victoria and Victor Hugo came here to take the air.

They stayed in the new town, christened Hyères-les-Palmiers by its creator Alexis Godillot. He owned half the town at the time, having made his money as an arms dealer. Designed by the architect Chapoulard, it is characterised by wide palm-lined avenues with harmonious Empire architecture, best seen on avenue Beauregard and avenue Rionet. Among the sumptuous 19th-century villas, the highlight is Villa Tunisienne on avenue Beauregard.

The charming old town clings to a rocky pinnacle a few hundred metres inland from the waterfront. Founded on the salt trade in the early Middle Ages, its now-silted port was an embarkation port for the Crusades. The counts of Provence ruled from a château above the town, but this was demolished during the reign of Louis XIII. The ruins are extensive and offer a panorama across the new town and coastline. In the lee of the castle is a maze of narrow streets and small squares leading back down the hill. Here you will wander past Romanesque and Renaissance houses to place Massillon, the main market square where Tour St-Blaise is all that remains of a 12th-century Templar commandery.

Although the town is a lively summer destination, it is also the centre of a thriving agricultural area, with palms being a major industry (there are several species called Hyères palms).

Take a ferry from Hyères port to the Îles d'Hyères (see p145) just offshore.

Presqu'île de Giens (Giens Peninsula)

Once an island, Giens is now attached to the mainland by not one but two 4km (2.5 mile) 'bars' of rock and sand called 'tombolos'. Either side of the tombolos, the shallow sea bays offer excellent conditions for windsurfing and sandy beaches amongst the tussocky grasses. Between the bars lie 400 hectares (1,000 acres) of salt marshes and the Étang des Pesquiers (Pesquiers Lake), one of the best places in the Riviera for birdwatchers.

Le Gros Cerveau

A series of hills rising inland between Toulon and Bandol, le Gros Cerveau has some of the last unspoilt *garrigue* (fragrant scrubland and pine forest) in the region. A narrow road snakes around the upper flanks of the mounts through landscapes heady with the smell of pine and wild herb and the drowsy humming of the *cigale* or cicada.

From here there are excellent panoramas of the western Varois coastline.

The road, the D220 reached from the town of Ollioules, is closed 1 July–15 Sept as a precaution against forest fires.

Mont Faron

High above Toulon, Mont Faron is considered the 'green lung' of the city. Though not the highest of the limestone hills that make up the Toulon range behind the city (it peaks at 584m or 1,916ft), it is the most accessible, by road or cable car, and city dwellers love to walk amongst the fragrant garrigue scrubland and pine woods.

The name Faron is derived from *faro* ('lighthouse' in the Provençal language) and the summit has a warning light and several eras' worth of fortifications. The panorama is spectacular, taking in Toulon, its *rade* (harbour) and much of the Varois coast.

Mont Faron also has an eclectic couple of attractions, a zoo – the only wild cat reproduction centre in Europe – and a museum set in the Tour Beaumont (Beaumont Tower) commemorating the 1944 allied landings in Provence.

Téléphérique (cable car), boulevard Amiral Vence. Tel: 04 94 92 68 25. Open: 9.30am–12pm, 2–6.30pm. Closed Mon and during high winds. Admission fee: combined ticket (cable car and zoo) or bus/boat/cable car pass. Museum of the Landing, Mont Faron. Tel: 04 94 88 08 09. Open: 9.45am–12.45pm, 1.45–4.30pm. Closed Mon. Admission fee. Mont Faron Zoo, Mont Faron.

Tel: 04 94 88 07 89. Open: daily, 2–6pm.
Closed on rainy days. Admission fee.

Toulon

Set on a majestic natural bay and backed by its eponymous mountains, Toulon has long been the French navy's largest base. Still home to aircraft carriers and submarines, Toulon has both benefited from its naval connection and suffered because of it, being attacked in several conflicts and badly damaged during the Second World War. Though you will have to ignore its rather unsightly docks and nondescript modern suburbs, Toulon has many attractions around the old town and its 19th-century annexes.

The city is named after the Celtic goddess Télo, patron of freshwater springs. During the 19th century it was given the genteel epithet 'city of fountains' for its 203 ornamental water sources, yet it was infamous for the heinous regime of its naval prison and its numerous brothels. Even today it has a certain *louche* appeal.

A one-hour boat tour of the Rade de Toulon (Toulon Bay) gives you a close view of the pride of the French Navy, plus all the other activities of the busy port. The naval base, begun in 1589 covers 268 hectares (662 acres), has 30km (19 miles) of roads and 12,000 employees, and is home to 30 ships. Tour boats depart from the Quai Cronstadt, a lively walkway lined with restaurants and cafés overlooking hundreds of small fishing boats, though rather spoiled by the dour concrete apartment blocks that replaced houses destroyed in the war.

The naval legacy of the town is celebrated in Musée National de la Marine (National Maritime Museum) in the form of

Tiny fishing boats crowd the harbour at Cassis

the 16th-century Tour Mitre (Mitre Tower), whose entrance is a monumental Renaissance stone portal. Displays include paintings, engravings, charts and model boats.

The oldest part of Toulon sits just inland from Quai Cronstadt. Characterised by tall three- and four-storey 18th- and 19th-century buildings, cut by narrow lanes and tiny squares, it is a bustling place, especially the large, colourful daily market on Cours Lafayette. The Musée de Vieux Toulon (Museum of Old Toulon) is here, in the old Bishop's Palace, with costumes, maps and paintings charting the history of the city.

La Cathédrale Ste-Marie-de-la-Seds is the last remnant of medieval Toulon. Built in the 11th century but with a 17th-century façade, it is almost veiled by a curtain of surrounding buildings. The very dark interior plays host to several paintings by Pierre Puget (1620–94), a sculptor and native of Marseille, in addition to a Baroque marble altar.

The old town is bounded to the north by the wide avenue du Maréchal Leclerc and boulevard de Strasbourg, on the site of the old city walls. These are lined with some excellent 19th-century buildings including the Théâtre/Opéra Municipal (1862) on the place Victor Hugo, and the Grand Hotel (1870) in place de la Liberté, where you will also find the monumental Fontaine de la Fédération, a fountain erected on the anniversary of the first French Republic in 1889.

Rade de Toulon: several companies offer tours. Admission fee: same for each company.

Musée National de la Marine, place Monsenergue, 83000 Toulon. Tel: 04 94 02 02 01. Open: 16 Sept–31 Mar, 10am–12pm, 2–6pm; 1 Apr–15 Sept, 10am–6pm. Closed Tue and 15 Dec–31 Jan. Admission fee.

Musée de Vieux Toulon, Cours Lafayette 69, 83000 Toulon. Tel: 04 94 62 11 07. Open: 2–5.45pm. Closed Sun and public holidays. Free.

ROYAL PURPLE

In Roman times, Toulon was an important supplier of Imperial Purple, one of the most prized natural pigments of its day. The dye was extracted from the glands of the conch (of the genus *stromidae*), which proliferated in these waters. It was steeped in a saline solution, then boiled for ten days in huge vats before being shipped to Rome, where it was used to dye silk for the imperial robes.

THE MODERN FRESCOES OF TOULON

Huge modern wall paintings are scattered about the centre of Toulon, celebrating the city's recent history and particular character: an epic card game is depicted in place Victor Hugo; the success of the merchant navy graces place Raimu; and daily life in 19th-century Toulon adorns the corner of rue Michelot.

Monumental frescoes illustrate Toulon's past

Walk: Central Toulon

This circular walk explores the centre, from 11th-century to 19th-century buildings by way of some of the town's major museums, through the narrow warren of streets that make up the old town.

Allow 2 hours.

Begin at the tourist office in place Raimu, where you can pick up information in English. Cross avenue de la République to reach the harbour.

1 Quai Cronstadt

This quayside promenade is bustling whatever time of day you arrive. Early in the day the fishermen are finishing their working day, the restaurants are busy at lunchtimes and all afternoon the cafés serve coffee to locals and tourists alike. Take a boat tour of the harbour from here.

Cross back over avenue de la République and turn right to the corner of Cours Lafayette, where you will take a left.

Quai Cronstadt makes a fine quayside promenade

2 The daily market

This fills Cours Lafayette and is one of the best along the coast (Monday's is a small market). You will find fresh fish, fruit, flowers plus clothing and practical crafts. It is the perfect place to watch locals buying their daily needs or for your picnic provisions.

At Cours Lafayette 69 you will find the Musée de Vieux Toulon. Here you can explore the history of the old town, its major triumphs and disasters.

Turn left at Traversée Cathédrale just in front of the museum and after 50m on the right, almost hidden behind the shop façades is Cathédrale Ste-Marie-de-la-Seds.

3 Cathédrale Ste-Marie-de-la-Seds

This mainly medieval building is the major place of worship for city-dwellers. The huge, dark interior, lit by hundreds of votive candles, has the feel of a cavern.

From the door of the cathedral, turn right and walk along rue Emile Zola into the heart of the old town. At rue d'Alger head right again to place C Ledeau, then follow rue Pierre Semard. A left at rue Nicolas Laugier will bring you to place du Globe.

4 Old Toulon

These streets form the heart of the old town; look up above the shop fronts to see typical Toulon domestic architecture. At place du Globe is Maison de la Photographie. This hosts temporary exhibitions by leading photographers on a variety of subjects.
On leaving the place du Globe, take a right to rue Nicolas Laugier and continue on rue de Pomet to place Victor Hugo.

5 Place Victor Hugo

This elegant square with its shady palms is home to the Théâtre/Opéra, a finely embellished Neoclassical design. It still has one of the finest 'seasons' in the Riviera.
Take rue Racine (left of the Théâtre) the short distance to boulevard de Strasbourg. Cross the street and walk left to place de la Liberte.

6 Place de la Liberté

There are excellent 19th-century buildings along boulevard de Strasbourg and avenue du Maréchal Leclerc, which runs into it. However, place de la Liberté offers the finest architectural vista, with the Grand Hotel and the Fontaine de la Fédération being particularly pleasing.
From the square, walk down rue Pastoureau, which continues as rue Anatole France, past the place d'Armes, commissioned by Colbert as a square to review troops, to place Monsenergue.

7 Musée National de la Marine

The fine portal, flanked by statues of Mars and Bellona, leads to rooms displaying a range of naval memorabilia, including model ships, paintings and statues of French admirals.
From the museum, return to Quai Cronstadt (left via avenue de la République) for refreshments.

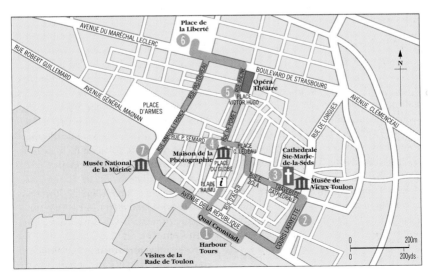

The Coast and the Massif des Maures

The ancient Maures hills offer some of the most fascinating landscapes and lifestyles along the Riviera. Still sparsely populated, they are blanketed with dense fragrant pine forest and wild herbs. Agriculture abounds in the form of vines, chestnuts and cork; local raw materials are still transformed into pottery or briar pipes using age-old techniques, yet amongst this rural idyll you will also find the most hip resort along the Riviera. If Cannes is where the stars come to work, St Tropez is where they let their hair down.

Wooden shutters protect against the strong Riviera sunlight

Bormes-les-Mimosas

Set on a verdant hillside just inland from the coast, Bormes-les-Mimosas is a typical Provençal village crowned by the remains of a medieval château. As its name would suggest, the village is surrounded by fragrant flower fields and this spills over into the town, where there is an abundance of blooms – not just mimosa, but jasmine, eucalyptus and potted geraniums.

The tangle of narrow old town lanes with several covered passageways and some exceptionally steep *chemins* or alleyways, the best of which is Rompi-Cou ('neck-breaker'), 183m (600ft) long with 83 narrow steps, now lined with tourist shops.

Église Saint-Trophyme (1775–8) is neo-Romanesque. The interior features 14 canvases by Alain Nonn depicting the Stations of the Cross. The inscription on the façade reads 'from everyday time to divine time'.

Just 100m (330ft) west of the village, Chapelle Saint-François de Paule was built in the 16th century in honour of the village's patron and renovated in the late 1980s. Most of the decoration and statuary is 19th century.

Bormes has a small Musée d'Arts et Histoire (Art and History Museum) with displays on the town and Chartreuse de la Verne (*see opposite*). It also has details of two local men who played an important part in South American history, Hippolyte Mourdeille (1758–1807), who routed the Spanish in Montevideo, and Hippolyte Bouchard (1780–1837), who developed the first Argentine naval units.

Musée d'Arts et Histoire, rue Carnot, 83230 Bormes-les-Mimosas. Tel: 04 94 71 56 60. Open: Mon–Sat 10am–12pm, 2.30–5pm, Sun 10am–12pm. Free.

Cap Camaret

A rocky outcrop forming the southern flank of the Baie de Pamplonne (where the prime St Tropez beaches lie), Cap Camaret is crowned by the Phare de Camaret (Camaret lighthouse), at 130m (426ft) one of the highest in France. The main attraction of the area is the walking, to the north with distant views across the bay or south to the unpopulated Cap Lardier peninsula where you find dramatic cliff views, the imposing Château de Volterra (not open to the public) and perhaps a native Hermann tortoise foraging in the *garrigue* or protected woodland.

Chartreuse de la Verne

Founded in 1170 in the heart of the Maures Forest by the Carthusians, this monastery is now the home of a community of nuns from the order of the Sisters of Bethlehem.

It is possible to tour part of the complex. Highlights include the 12th-century kitchen and the cloisters. Local

The lighthouse at Cap Camaret is one of the tallest in France

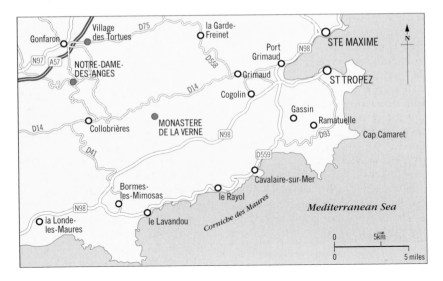

stone has been used throughout. Brown schist for the walls is enhanced by a blue/green serpentine for the lintels, door-frames and interior arches.

Take the RD14 road towards Grimaud and the convent is signposted down a side road. Tel: 04 94 48 08 00. Open: summer 11am–6pm, winter 11am–5pm. Closed: Tue in January and during religious celebrations. Free.

Cogolin

This parish retains its traditional artisans and skilled craftsmen. It is here that you will still be able to watch pipe makers, workers of cork and potters at their workshops, or rug weavers.

Though surrounded by modern suburbs, the heart of the town is l'Église St Sauveur with its 20th-century triptych, as well as the Tour Horloge,

with remnants of the old town walls, and a castle. Chapelle St-Roch on the outskirts was built in the 17th century by plague survivors.

Cogolin was the final home of Raimu (the stage name of Jules Muraire), the famous French actor. A small museum features photographs of Raimu, some of his costumes and many of his personal effects.

Musée Espace Raimu, avenue Georges Clémenceau 18, 83310 Cogolin. Tel: 04 94 54 18 00, www.musee-raimu.com. Open: winter 10am–12pm, 3–6pm; summer 10am–12pm, 4–7pm. Closed: Fri am. Admission fee.

Collobrières

Collobrières is the agricultural 'capital' of this rural Massif des Maures, and the centre of the largest collection of

Escape on foot into the Maures mountains

A 12th-century bridge spans the river at Collobrières

megalithic remains in the region. The major crop here is *marron* ('chestnut') from the surrounding *chataigne* ('chestnut') forests. Between October and December you can sample delicious hot chestnuts straight from the brazier but the rest of the year products include chestnut paste, jam, liqueur, ice cream and chocolates, and preserved fruits. Oak is also a major crop and you will see the 'stripped' barks on trees on the approach road.

The town, whose name is derived from the Latin 'Collubriera' meaning 'grass snake', sits astride the Réal Collobrier River, connected by a simple 12th-century bridge. You can wander around the old *usine de liège* ('cork factory') that until 1960 produced stoppers for the wine industry, or walk up to the dilapidated Romanesque church.

Le Domaine du Rayol

Domaine du Rayol is the finest estate in this part of the Riviera. Sitting amongst abundant natural pine forest next to the rocky coastline, it recreates gardens of the world that have a Mediterranean climate, with cacti from Mexico, bamboo from China and plants from the Canary Islands, California, Chile and South Africa.
Avenue des Belges, 83820 Le Rayol-Canadel. Tel: 04 98 04 44 00.
www.domainedurayol.org

Open: Apr–Sept 9.30am–12.30pm,
2.30–6.30pm; Feb–Mar & Oct–Nov
9.30am–12.30pm, 2–5.30pm. Closed:
Mon and 22 Nov–24 Jan. Admission fee.

La Garde-Freinet

Set in a wide valley in the midst of the
Maures Massif, La Garde-Freinet thrived
on silk, olive oil, cork and cork products
in the 19th century (though there are no
signs of it today).

Above the village, lonely walls and
stone staircases betray the 12th-century
fort carved out of the rocky 450m
(1,476ft) summit, but the site is an
active archaeological dig and has yet to
reveal all its secrets.

Sampling chestnut products of the Maures

Another marked walk leads to La
Roches Blanches. From a distance these
rocks look like snow-capped peaks, but
are in fact outcrops of white quartz
reaching 638m (2,093ft).

Gassin

Above this 13th-century village is
the highest point of the St Tropez
peninsula, Dëi Barri, with 360° views
over St Tropez and its beaches, inland
towards the Maures and south to
Le Lavandou and the Varois Coast.

The village was long a centre of
traditional crafts, but today is given over
to galleries and shops. The architectural
renovations (plus building of a modern
quarter), undertaken by François
Spoerry of Port Grimaud fame, have
received the prestigious *Marianne d'Or*
award, but lovers of the 'slightly faded
glory' found in other Provençal villages
may be disappointed by the pristine
paintwork and stucco.

Highlights of a village tour include
Notre Dame de l'Assomption,
completed in 1558 and home to a
venerated statue of the village patron
Saint Laurent, and rue Rompe, a little
alleyway reputed to be the narrowest in
the world.

Grimaud

A typical feudal medieval village,
Grimaud retains its old-world charm,
with a series of narrow lanes flanked by
tall stone houses bedecked with vines
and flowers leading up to the remains of
a summit-top château.

Within the village there are several
churches worth visiting. Chapelle des
Pénitents, also called Notre Dame des

Sept Douleurs (1482), houses the shrines of St Théodore and St Lambert, whilst Notre Dame le la Queste, home to a fine Louis XVI altar, is the site of a blessing of horses and mules on 16 August. Église St Michel dates mainly from the 10th century.

The highlight of secular architecture is the 16th-century La Maison des Templiers, with Renaissance arches and a fully working 17th-century flour mill.

Le Lavandou

Excellent beaches are the attraction of Le Lavandou, the major tourist resort of the western Maures. It has over a dozen named strands, each with its own character, including plage du Rossignol and plage du Layet, both naturist beaches. The town itself still has a Provençal character (though no major monuments) and good modern facilities for holiday-makers.

Notre-Dame-des-Anges has been a place of pilgrimage since the 11th century

Port Grimaud

The Riviera's 'little Venice', Port Grimaud is a modern and totally artificial settlement built in Provençal style during the late 1960s in marshland at the head of the Golfe de Saint Tropez (Gulf of St Tropez). The concept for a water-based settlement evoking the traditions of the region was the brainchild of architect François Spoerry who used the latest innovative construction methods to dig the canals, drain and reclaim the land.

Today Port Grimaud is a carefully planned and sculpted *mélange* of pastel Provençal-style terraced houses and apartments, interspersed with 7km (4 miles) of canals for yachts and small boats. Vehicular traffic is carefully controlled, making it a pleasure to stroll around the small squares hosting shops, cafés and restaurants, especially atmospheric in the evenings.

Ramatuelle

Overlooking the glorious beaches of St Tropez in the Baie de Pamplonne, the labyrinthine alleyways of the village of Ramatuelle offer a wealth of medieval detail set amidst ancient ramparts. Porte Sarrasine (Saracen Gate) with its portcullis locked in position is the major entryway; also part of the walls is Église Notre-Dame – the bell tower acted as a lookout – with an unusual serpentine portal of 1620. At the heart of the settlement is place de l'Ormeau, shaded by olive trees.

Look out for the modern monument to French submariners of 1939–45, designed by Coubier (1959). It stands here because a resistance cell from Ramatuelle helped the submariners.

Like other medieval settlements, Ramatuelle has a community of artists and its associated galleries.

On a hilltop high above the village and perfectly placed to catch the sea breezes lie Les Moulins de Paillas, three windmills (in working order until *c.* 1900), one of them fully restored.

Sainte Maxime

Created as recently as 1790 with the amalgamation of two *seigneuries* ('feudal settlements'), Ste Maxime is now one of the most popular modern resorts along the Riviera. It is much more low-key than, say, Cannes or neighbouring St Tropez. It hosts a large pleasure port and is surrounded by good beaches, making it popular with families and a useful base from which to explore the area.

There are few historic remains although Tour Carrée of 1520, built as a defence against pirates, marks the entrance to an old town where you will find the parish church of 1762 with iron bell tower, a well, and 18th-century *lavoirs* (public wash houses) on rue Hoche. The tower houses the Musée des Traditions Locales (Museum of Local Traditions), displaying Provençal costumes, tools and fishing objects.

The family of writer Guy de Maupassant owned La Villa Bethanie and he spent some time in the town. *Musée des Traditions Locales, avenue Charles de Gaulle, 83120 Sainte-Maxime. Tel: 04 94 96 70 30. Open: Sept–June 10am–12pm, 3–6pm; July–Aug 10am–12pm, 3–7pm. Closed: Mon am and Tue. Admission fee.*

Saint Tropez

Discovered by the 'arty' élite at the start of the 20th century, when painter Paul Signac sailed his yacht into the harbour, St Tropez has experienced a sea-change in both its fortune and its character. It was rediscovered by director Roger Vadim in the 1950s and his young star Brigitte Bardot took the tiny fishing village to her heart. The cream of French and Hollywood cinema arrived in their droves, followed since then by supermodels, pop stars and assorted *jeunesse dorée*. They all come to enjoy the relaxed atmosphere of the town and the fantastic beaches on the Ramatuelle peninsula.

The artists of today display their canvases on the quayside, on the western flank of the port, adding extra interest to the compulsory evening harbour stroll, as buyers compare techniques and prices. However the deconsecrated Chapelle Notre-Dame de l'Annonciade (built *c.* 1568) houses the Musée de Saint Tropez, a veritable digest of early 20th-century art, featuring Braque, Dufy, Maillol, Matisse, Seurat and Signac himself with *Saint Tropez, l'Orage* (1895), showing the port in a storm. This harbour still protects a small fishing fleet, but also plays host to the élite of the yachting world, with several important regattas each year and a resident fleet of large sailing boats and floating gin-palaces.

Around the harbour, the pastel houses have long since passed from fishing families into the hands of restaurants, galleries and up-market shops, but again the atmosphere is low-key. The Ponche district to the east of the harbour has

The Riviera's 'little Venice', Port Grimaud offers the perfect waterside lifestyle

some excellent domestic architecture and a 19th-century Italian Baroque church with typical wrought iron bell-tower, where you will find the venerated statue of St Tropez, patron of the town.

Though the place was founded before the birth of Jesus and was settled in the Roman era, the citadel is the oldest building still standing in the town. Construction began in 1602 with the central *donjon* or keep, but the fort saw action in 1637 and 1707 (both times against the Spanish) and it was expanded through the 18th century. Within the *donjon*, the Musée Naval (Naval Museum) displays a number of scale models, charts and navigational instruments, plus a gallery devoted to the Allied landings in Provence in 1944.

Though visitors gravitate towards the harbour side, locals make their way to the large place des Lices for café society, turning the morning marketplace into a vast *boulodrome* each early evening.

St Tropez hosts two *bravades* ('acts of defiance') each year. The first sees the statue of the town's patron (a Christian centurion, beheaded for his faith in Pisa on the orders of Emperor Nero, whose pristine remains floated ashore in the bay of St Tropez) carried triumphantly around the town (17 May). The second (15 June) marks the date in 1637 when local inhabitants vanquished the Spanish.

Musée de Saint Tropez, place Grammont, 83990 Saint Tropez. Tel: 04 94 97 04 01. Open: 1 June–30 Sept 10am–12pm, 3–9pm; 1 Oct–31 May 10am–12pm, 2–6pm. Closed: Nov, 1 Jan, 1 May, Ascension Day and Christmas Day. Admission fee.

Citadel Saint Tropez/Musée Naval, 83990 Saint Tropez. Tel: 04 94 97 59 43. Open: 1 Oct–31 Mar 10am–12.30pm, 1.30–5.30pm; 1 Apr–30 Sept 10am–12.30pm, 1.30–6.30pm. Closed: 1 Jan, 1 May, 17 May,

Shady café in Port Grimaud

Ascension Day, 1 Nov, 11 Nov and
Christmas Day. Admission fee.

Sanctuaire Notre-Dame-des-Anges (Sanctuary of Our Lady of the Angels)

Now in the care of the Franciscan friars
of the Immaculate Conception, the
sanctuary housing the revered statue of
Notre Dame des Anges has a long
history, though the present church dates
from only 1853. The earliest mention
of a religious site here can be found
in a decree from Thierry, son of the
Merovingian King Clovis, in 517. It
was a priory of Augustinian canons
until the Revolution.

The cult of Our Lady developed
through vox-pop. In the 11th century
a local shepherd was drawn to the
statue by the baying of hounds. It was

Fishing for tonight's dinner?

installed in a local church but would
'miraculously' find its way back to its
point of discovery. It was soon on
medieval pilgrimage routes, the focus of
prayer for the ill and the desperate. The
statue is said to have saved the people of
Pignans from the plague in 1720 and a
severe drought in 1723.

Though the church is rather plain, it
is overflowing with fascinating votive
offerings, from paintings, embroideries
and model ships to depictions of limbs
and crutches, attesting to the strong
faith of pilgrims even in modern times.

There are excellent views of the
Maures hills from the courtyard outside
the church.

Sanctuaire Notre-Dame-des-Anges,
83790 Pignans. Tel: 04 94 59 00 69.
Open: 8.45am–8pm. Free. Suitable
clothing required.

AND GOD CREATED WOMAN – THE RISE AND RISE OF BRIGITTE BARDOT.

When Roger Vadim directed the
provocative *And God Created Woman*
in 1956, he chose a demure blonde French
actress Brigitte Bardot for the lead role. When
the film was released, this coquettish young
woman exploded onto the world stage,
becoming the embodiment of female teenager
as James Dean did for males.

However, the intensely private Bardot tired
of the movie scene and began to find the
constant attention suffocating. She eventually
retired from films to her villa La Madrague on
the Ramatuelle peninsula in 1973 to devote
herself to animal welfare and occasionally to
be glimpsed in St Tropez.

Le Village des Tortues
(Tortoise Village)

A kind of 'Noah's Ark' for the Hermann tortoise, the village rescues injured animals (up to 100 a year), fosters a breeding colony (releasing up to 500 juveniles into the wild each year) and promotes the welfare of these creatures, acting as a centre of excellence.

There are hundreds of the cute prehistoric throwbacks on display, from 3cm (1¼ in) one-year-olds to fully-grown adults and you can view the quarantine tanks, breeding colony and a selection of other tortoises from around the world.

In summer, visit early or late in the day as tortoises take a siesta during the afternoon heat.

Le Village des Tortues, 83590 Gonfaron (on the D75 east of the village).
Tel: 04 94 78 26 41. www.tortues.com.
Open: daily 9am–7pm. Closed: Mar–Nov.
Admission fee.

THE MAURES TORTOISE

Mainland France's only native tortoise population can be found in the Massif des Maures, though numbers are under threat and it has been a protected species since 1985.

Known as Hermann's tortoise, the species has roamed the area for 35 million years. It is perfectly adapted to life in the dry forests and has a lifespan of up to 80 years, though over a third of this time is spent hibernating in a warm hollow tree-trunk or hole.

Newly hatched tortoises are only a few centimetres (1–2in) long and are preyed on by magpies, buzzards, foxes and even hedgehogs, but the encroachment of man is the main threat to their survival.

Pastel-hued houses line the waterfront at St Tropez

The place to be young and cool

FOREST FIRES

Devastating fires during the summer of 2003 destroyed hundreds of hectares of forest. Such fires threaten the future of the wild areas of the Riviera.

In summer, forest floors become tinder-dry but basic precautions will minimise the risk of wild fires. Do not discard lighted cigarettes into dry undergrowth by flicking them out of your car window. Do not set fires in woodland and only barbeque in designated areas, making sure to douse the hot coals before you leave. Do not leave litter (dry paper can burn easily) or broken bottles, which can magnify the sun's rays to ignite dry grasses or twigs.

Relax at a harbour-front café

Drive: Touring the Massif des Maures

This circular drive takes in the great contrasts of the Maures, the verdant forested peaks, hectares of chestnut forests, medieval hilltop villages, resorts and towns, offering a comprehensive picture of this relatively unspoilt corner of the Riviera.

Allow 8 hours.

Leave St Tropez on the D98A, following signs for Port Grimaud on the N98. Park in the Port Grimaud car park.

1 Port Grimaud
This is the 'Little Venice' of the Riviera, a man-made neo-Provençal village built in the 1960s around a series of canals. Its small plazas linked by narrow bridges make the perfect place for strolling amongst the pastel-hued buildings.
From Port Grimaud, take the D14 inland to Grimaud.

2 Grimaud
Grimaud is the older sibling of Port Grimaud and is a splendid medieval village once owned by the Grimaldi family and crowned by their fortified château. Make sure you see the fine façade of the Maison des Templiers on rue des Templiers.
From Grimaud, head northwest on

the D558 over the Maures hills to La Garde-Freinet.

Harvested cork for sale in the Maures

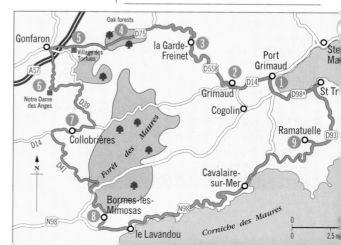

3 La Garde-Freinet

This sleepy village stands in the shadow
of its ruined citadel. It is a somnolent
place, especially after the bustle of St
Tropez, but acts as a base for a number
of marked footpaths.

*North of La Garde-Freinet, continue on
the D558 until its junction with the D75.
Here you will turn left signposted
Gonferon and les Mayons.*

4 La Garde-Freinet to Gonfaron

The D75 leads through a shallow valley
between the two Maures ranges.
Sparsely populated, here you will find
numerous cork oak forests – the bark
of the trees regularly 'harvested' and the
trunks painted with fungicide to guard
against disease.

*After 12km (7.5 miles) on the D75 you will
come to the Village des Tortues on the left.*

5 Le Village des Tortues

This is both a sanctuary and breeding
colony for the Hermann tortoise, a native
Maures species. You can observe and
learn about this fascinating creature.

*From the Village des Tortues, continue on
the D75 towards Gonfaron (left out of the
car park). When the D75 meets the D39,
go straight across the junction on a minor
RF road, direction Notre Dame des Anges.
After 9.5km (15 miles), turn right at the
junction of the GR9.*

6 Notre Dame des Anges

This has been a place of pilgrimage since
the 11th century. Take time to study the
hundreds of votive offerings inside,
then enjoy the panoramic view from
the courtyard.

*Return to the GR9 and follow it until it
reaches the junction of the D39 (direction
Col du Fourches). Here turn right in the
direction of Collobrières.*
*Warning: at times of high fire risk, the
roads to Notre Dame des Anges are closed.
In this event take a left where the D75
meets the D39, bringing you directly to
Collobrières.*

7 Collobrières

This section of the drive is the most
dramatic of the trip, with hectares of
thick native forest and switchback roads
offering distant views towards the coast.
As you near Collobrières, chestnuts
become the predominant crop and you
can taste chestnut (*marron*) products
in the town.

*Leave Collobrières on the D14, then turn
left at its junction with the D41 in the
direction of Bormes-les-Mimosas.*

8 Bormes-les-Mimosas

Explore this medieval 'village of flowers'
with its narrow, arcaded passageways.

*From Bormes-les-Mimosas, travel south
in the direction of Le Lavandou on the
D559, through a series of small coastal
resorts to la Croix-Valmer. Here, turn
right at the junction with the D93 into
the vine-blanketed St Tropez peninsula.
At the D61, turn left to Ramatuelle.*

9 Ramatuelle

Take time to walk through the portcullis
gateway and explore the narrow
medieval alleyways of this artists'
enclave.

*Return to the D93 and travel north (left)
back to St Tropez.*

St Tropez has, without doubt, the most racy reputation on the Côte d'Azur. The birthplace of topless sunbathing, its beaches have become a byword for sensual self-indulgence, fuelled by the antics of its celebrity guests. The rich and famous come to hang out, literally, at the *guinguettes* or beach bars that fringe the golden sands.

It is difficult to imagine now, as you pass your third Ferrari within a few

hundred yards, that in 1955 the area around St Tropez was one of the most remote parts of the coast. Ramatuelle and Gassin were somnolent, careworn villages surrounded by vineyards, still marking time with the harvest rather than the clock, while Pampelonne Bay was a natural wonderland of pine forest and scrub without water or electricity, the sublime arc of golden sand totally undeveloped. It was the simple beauty of the location that drew Roger Vadim for the film *And God Created Woman* starring the little-known actress Brigitte Bardot.

The first beach bars started life as caterers to the film production crew. One French explorer who had bought a large plot of land by the bay organised lunch each day, while fisherman Felix opened a small bar. Whether they realised quite how the film would change their lives and the life of St Tropez is open to question, but once the film hit cinemas the world wanted to own Brigitte – and, since she was drawn to St Tropez, so were they.

First Brigitte with Roger Vadim, then Brigitte with Gunther Sachs, spent their free time at the old crew lunch spot – now christened Club 55 – on Plage de Pampelonne (Pampelonne Beach) or at Plage Tahiti, Felix's place, surrounded by a coterie of hedonistic pals. More stars followed, Sophia Loren and Carlo Ponti, the Rolling Stones, Elizabeth Taylor and Richard Burton all added an extra frisson

of glamour. By now the beach bars had become almost resorts in themselves with swimming pools, sunbeds, restaurants, shops, plus security that kept the paparazzi at bay.

Today, both these establishments are still major players on the celebrity circuit. Club 55 is *the* place for celebrity lunching (*Tel: 04 94 55 55 55, only open 12–6pm*) while Tahiti Beach (*Tel: 04 94 97 18 02*) – nicknamed 'Beach of the Stars' – is the place to tan, though most superstars never venture near the water because it is much too public. Le Voile Rouge, where you tread in the footsteps of Jean-Paul Gaultier, has quite a reputation for uproarious behaviour and the 'new kid on the block' is Nikki Beach (*Tel: 04 94 79 82 04*), where Naomi Campbell had her birthday party in 2003.

After hours, Les Caves du Roy (*Tel: 04 95 56 68 00*) at the Byblos Hotel is where you will share the dance floor with Elton John, Mick Jagger or P Diddy, plus a plethora of minor names.

You will need to book ahead at all these places, especially in summer. Sunbed rental costs about 20 euros per day, not bad considering you may find your face on the pages of *Hello!* magazine, shaking hands with your favourite celeb!

Opposite: The bikini was invented in France
Above: Share some serious relaxation with a few superstars at a St Tropez beach bar

Inland to the Haut-Var

The Haut-Var is where the Riviera meets rural France, where the legions of tourists begin to dissipate a little and life moves at a slower pace, revolving more around agriculture and the seasons. The landscape offers a mantle of shimmering olive groves dotted with tiny communities and riven by dramatic gorges, which offer the perfect environment for action sports such as climbing and white-water rafting.

Ripening vines near Les Arcs

Les Arcs

Epicentre of the Côtes de Provence wine production region, les Arcs was the fiefdom of the Villeneuve family. Le Parage, their medieval demesne atop the village, has been fully renovated and now consists of a handful of family homes and a hotel/restaurant. This is where Sainte Roseline de Villeneuve was born (*see Chapelle Ste-Roseline p61*).

In the village, the parish church contains a *polyptych* (painted altarpiece in a series of hinged leaves) by Louis Bréa, painted in 1501, and a series of frescoes depicting scenes from the life of Sainte Roseline.

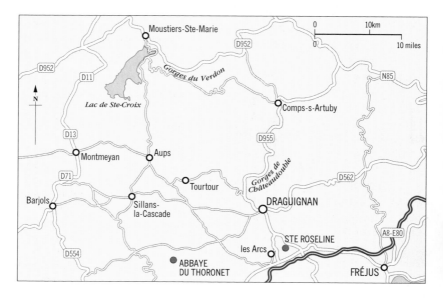

Cascade de Sillans

The 20m (66ft) drop of the Sillans waterfall may not match Niagara Falls but it is one of the region's natural wonders. The flow of the River Bresque drops abruptly over the edge of the rock face into azure pools surrounded by lush vegetation. It is a 2.5km (1.5 mile) walk from the car park and the last few metres of the path have been eroded by the footfalls of visitors, so do keep a tight hold of young children.

The tiny village of Sillans was founded in the 11th century and still displays sections of its medieval curtain wall, though the castle has long since vanished.

Waterfall open: all hours (but the path is not lit, so it is not advisable to visit after dark). Free.

Draguignan

The largest town of the Var hinterland, Draguignan is the home of the army's artillery school and the Musée de l'Artillerie, with its collection of cannons, munitions and field weapons. Life-size dioramas depict First World War munitions in action and a military camp of 1939–45.

The busy town centre is characterised by wide tree-lined boulevards, laid down during the 19th century when the city was prefectural capital of the Var (a status passed later to Toulon) and designed by Baron Haussman, who changed the face of Paris. There is still an atmospheric old quarter to explore, marked by two intact medieval gates – Porte des Portaiguières and Porte Romaine.

Highlights of the district are Tour de l'Horloge, built in 1660 on the site of the castle keep, and a 13th-century synagogue. The 'flamboyant-Gothic' Chapelle Notre-Dame-du-Peuple was erected in the 16th century in thanks to the Virgin for saving the town from the plague. The interior is teeming with votive offerings and the population hold a solemn pilgrimage on 8 September each year.

Draguignan also has two interesting museums. The Musée Municipal has some valuable ceramics from France and the Far East, and the art gallery contains

Mature olive trees may be centuries old

pieces by Rembrandt, Frans Hals and
J-B Van Loo.

The Musée des Traditions Provençales
offers an excellent insight into rural life
in this region, including viniculture,
milling, olive-oil production, cork
harvesting and industries such as
ceramics and glass-blowing.

*Musée de l'Artillerie, 83007 Draguignan
(on the D59 on the outskirts of town).
Tel: 04 98 10 83 85. Open: Sun–Wed
9am–12pm, 1.30–5.30pm. Free.
Musée Municipal, rue de la Republic 9,
80300 Draguignan. Tel: 04 98 10 26 85.
Open: Mon–Sat 9am–12pm, 2–6pm. Free.
Musée des Traditions Provençales,
rue Roumanille, 83007 Draguignan.
Tel: 04 94 47 05 72. Open: 9am–12pm,
2–6pm. Closed: Sun am and Mon.
Admission fee.*

Gorges de Châteaudouble

The River Naturby has carved a deep
gorge that snakes through the foothills
of the Haut-Var just north of
Draguignan. The chasm narrows as you
drive through it, offering excellent views
up the sheer side-walls, and there are
prehistoric caves to explore, though you
will need to reach them on foot.

Dramatic views of its meandering
path and the verdant peaks surrounding
it can be had from the terrace or
the Saracen Tower in the village of
Châteaudouble, which stands 100m
(330ft) above the gorge at the northern
end.

Gorges du Verdon

The most spectacular gorge in Europe
lies along the path of the Verdon River
on the northern boundary of the

Elegant façades in Draguignan

Riviera. A chasm some 700m (2,500ft)
deep has been carved out of the
limestone rock over the aeons.

The gorge is best seen by following
the signposted 'route des Crêtes' to the
north making sure to stop at the Point
Sublime for the most accessible grand
view, or the Corniche Sublime to the
south. Much better, however, to take to
the footpaths above the gorge top or
along its floor to really feel at one with
the landscape. The gorge is also excellent
for more energetic sports, from kayaking
to mountain climbing.

Le Musée de Préhistoire des Gorges
du Verdon (Museum of Prehistory of

the Verdon Gorge), 50km (30 miles) to the west, is the largest museum of prehistory in Europe and brings together material from over 60 sites to explain the history of man in Haute-Provence and recreate an ancient settlement.

Le Musée de Préhistoire des Gorges du Verdon, route de Montmayan, 04500 Quinson. Tel: 04 92 74 09 59, www.museeprehistoire.com. Open: 1 Feb–31 Mar, 10am–6pm; 1 Apr–30 June, 10am–7pm; 1 July–31 Aug, 10am–8pm; 1 Sept–30 Sept, 10am–7pm; 1 Oct–14 Dec, 10am–6pm. Closed: 15 Dec–31 Jan and Tue. Admission fee.

Chapelle Ste-Roseline

One of the finest chapels on the Riviera, Chapelle Ste-Roseline displays over 500 years' worth of exceptional religious art, including a mosaic by Marc Chagall.

Once part of the 11th-century Abbaye de la Celle Roubaud where Sainte Roseline de Villeneuve (of noble birth from Les Arcs) was mother superior in the early 1400s. Completed in 1200 in archetypal Romanesque style (in the shape of a Latin cross, with thick low walls, vaulting and simple semi-circular arches), the chapel remained consecrated ground after the sale of the surrounding monastic lands in 1793 and was bought

L'Abbaye du Thoronet is one of the finest examples of Romanesque architecture in France

by the commune of Les Arcs in 1829. The body of the saint lies in repose on the right of the nave, dressed in her simple habit.

The chapel is divided by a fine rood screen (choir screen) of 1638, surmounted by a statue of Saint Catherine of Alexandria. The ornate choir stalls are 20 years younger.

The main altar displays a hand-carved reredos (ornamental screen behind the altar) donated by Louis III, then Count of Provence. It features a *Descent from the Cross* (1514).

Stone steeples punctuate the skyline

On the left of the nave, a second reredos is dedicated to St Antony of Padua and decorated with a renowned *predella* (painting decorating the altar).

Marc Chagall was invited to make his own mark on the chapel during renovation funded by the Maeght family (*for their art collection, see St Paul de Vence, pp93–6*). His monumental mosaic *Le Repas des Anges* ('Meal of the Angels') of 1975 depicts Ste Roseline's life here as a novice. Her miraculous 'still-living eyes' are set in a glass reliquary with bronze doors by Diego Giacommetti (1975).

The old monastery lands are now part of the award-winning Sainte-Roseline vineyard next to the chapel, where you can taste their new wines.
Chapelle Ste Roseline, 83460 Les Arcs (on the D91 west of the town). Tel: 04 94 73 37 30 (tourist information, Les Arcs). Open: 10am–12pm, 2–6pm. Free.

L'Abbaye du Thoronet

One of the finest Cistercian complexes in France and one of three such abbeys in Provence, the abbey was founded *c.* 1160 on land presented to the order by Raymond Béranger, Marquis de Provence. It went into decline as early as the 14th century, but in 1854 it was saved by Prosper Mérimée, who suggested that the French state buy the site.

The ensemble is a masterpiece of Romanesque architecture, with simple lines and minimal ornament. The interior of the church has a low, vaulted ceiling and rounded windows. The cloisters are, unusually, built on a gradient. Once again, vaulted ceilings are in evidence. The west gallery has a display of illuminated manuscripts.

The domestic area of the abbey complex is the only place you will find any form of decoration. The Chapter House is built in later Gothic style, with pillars and vaulted ceiling. Above it is the monk's dormitory.

L'Abbaye du Thoronet, 83340 Le Thoronet. Tel: 04 94 60 43 90, www.monum.fr. Open: 1 Apr–30 Sept, Mon–Sat 10am–6.30pm, Sun 10am–12pm, 2–6.30pm; 1 Oct–31 Mar, Mon–Sat 10am–1pm, 2–5pm, Sun 10am–12pm, 2–5pm. Closed: 1 Jan, 1 May, 1 Nov, 11 Nov, Christmas Day. Admission fee.

Medieval arcaded alley in Tourtour

Tourtour

On the site of a 12th-century Cistercian abbey, this medieval village nestles amongst the remains of a fortified château. One of the most fashionable in the area with the 'arty' crowd, its vaulted passageways and narrow winding alleyways are lined with renovated 17th-century stone houses, now home to numerous galleries.

At the heart of town is the 16th-century Tour de l'Horloge (clock tower) and a 17th-century olive mill.

Just beyond the citadel walls, there are exceptional views from the grassy knoll where stands l'Église St Denis, an 11th-century Romanesque church rebuilt in the 19th century. A viewing table points out landmarks and lower villages. If it is clear you can see the Maures, the Luberon, Ste Baume and Mont Ste Victoire near Aix-en-Provence. Tourtour is nicknamed the '*village dans le ciel*' or village in the sky.

TRUFFLES

Known as 'black gold' in France, the truffle – a fungus that grows in the roots of oak trees – is one of the most sought-after and valuable ingredients in *haute cuisine*.

Of the two varieties, white and black, it is the black truffle that is most prized for its flavour and aroma. It ripens in the autumn and its distinctive scent is picked up by the 'truffling' dogs or pigs trained to sniff it out.

Look for fresh truffles on sale in the markets during the winter. During the remainder of the year you can buy preserved truffles or oil infused with truffles.

Drive: Discovering the Haut-Var

This circular tour passes innumerable small villages scattered across the landscape of the Haut-Var, taking in the Abbey du Thoronet and Chapelle Ste-Roseline. Although there are restaurants along the way, a picnic would be a great way to enhance your tour, stopping at one of the great viewpoints.

Allow 6 hours.

Start from Draguignan on the D955, northwards.

1 Gorges de Châteaudouble
These gorges are a micro eco-system; rocky, marshy and forested, with waterfalls and rock pools..

Turn left at the junction of the D51 into Châteaudouble village.

2 Châteaudouble
This tiny village has a small tangle of streets and a terrace with pretty views over the gorge from above. The restaurant here offers local specialities,

The winding road through the Gorges de Châteaudouble

especially in winter (ingredients such as truffles and wild boar).

Leave Châteaudouble and continue on the D51 to Ampus.

3 Ampus
Ampus is a tiny medieval village with an 11th-century church in the old part of the village. On the site of the old château are a series of ceramic tableaux of the last days of Christ by Geoff, erected in 1985.

From Ampus take the D51 through St Pierre-de-Tourtour (not at all exciting) to Tourtour. There is a great view as you approach the town.

4 Tourtour
Standing at an altitude of 625m (2,050ft), this medieval village has panoramic views across the southern Var from the viewing table outside the 11th-century Église St-Denis. Visit the fossil museum in the Tour de l'Horloge.

From Tourtour, continue on the D51 through Villecroze and on to Salernes renowned as a producer of ceramic tiles. Take the D560 out of the town to Sillans-la-Cascade.

5 Sillans-la-Cascade

This 20m (66ft) water-chute sits in a wooded valley, but it is a 2.5km (1.5 mile) walk, taking an hour out of your trip. The final approach is steep and unpaved and a visit in wet weather is not recommended.
Proceed south on the D22 to Cotignac. There is a great view of the terracotta roofs of the old town set below the overhanging rock face and the remains of two medieval towers. Take the D13 to Carcès at the confluence of the Argens and Cassolle rivers, and continue through the village for 2km (1¼ miles), where you will take a left on the D279, signposted Abbaye du Thoronet. After 8.5km (5¼ miles) you will reach the abbey.

6 Abbaye du Thoronet

The abbey was built by the Cistercians in the 12th century and has some fine Romanesque architecture. Next door, the monks of the Monastère de Bethléem make their own pottery, on sale at their gift shop.
Leave the abbey on the D19, direction le Thoronet. Once there, turn left on the

D17 and cross the River Argens to reach Lorgues, where the huge Eglise Collégiale St Martin de Lorgues (built in the early 1700s) dominates the skyline. From Lorgues take the D10 to les Arcs.

7 les Arcs

Climb through the lower section of the village to view the tiny medieval enclave of Parage, beautifully renovated ancestral home of the Villeneuve family (Sainte Roseline was a Villeneuve). There is an excellent restaurant/hotel.
Take the D91 to the Chapelle Ste-Roseline.

8 Chapelle Ste-Roseline

This 12th-century chapel houses the reliquary of Sainte Roseline. The beautiful 16th-century decoration is augmented by a 20th-century ceramic masterpiece by Marc Chagall. Next to the chapel is the Ste-Roseline vineyard, where you can try some of the estate-bottled wines after your visit.
From here head back to Draguignan on the D91 and N555.

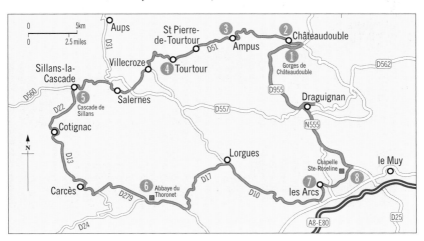

We are all searching for the perfect diet, something to keep us healthy and youthful. Well, doctors and dieticians all agree that two staples of the southern French diet, olive oil and wine, form important ingredients of this magic elixir.

Olive oil

Olive oil contains the most digestible of all oils. It does not modify digestive juices, and contains low levels of polyunsaturates and acidity, so reducing the build-up of cholesterol and the risk of heart disease, thrombosis and arteriosclerosis.

But it has got to be the right kind of olive oil. The oil is in the flesh of the olives, so they must be crushed. Traditionally this was done in a mill between heavy stones. The resulting paste was spread on grass mats called *scourtins*, which were then piled together and pressed with a great weight to release the oil. In modern mills, the process is similar but the millstones have gone to museums while the *scourtins* have been replaced by metal disks.

Among these 'cold pressed' oils, the first pressing is called 'extra-virgin' – the best quality with the most health benefits. A second pressing results in 'virgin' olive oil, but each successive pressing reduces the flavour and the health benefits. Always look for 'extra-virgin' on the label to ensure quality.

Wine

The positive benefits, particularly for red wine, are now well documented – elimination of free radicals, lowering of blood pressure, reducing heart disease and controlling the effects of bronchitis amongst others – as long as you do not drink too much! Much of the benefit comes from the grape skins left in the juice of red wine, unlike white wine

and *rosé* (where they are squeezed during wine pressing but not left in the maturing mixture, hence the *rosé* or 'pink' colour).

The hot dry summers of the Riviera are not conducive to the production of very fine, long-lived wines such as the Grand Crus of Bordeaux or Burgundy, but their younger, fruitier wines are perfect to accompany a long alfresco lunch or as an evening aperitif. Best choices are *rosé* from around Bandol, made mainly from the *mourdèvre* grape not commonly used in other wine producing areas. You will also find quaffable wines on the Ramatuelle peninsula south of St Tropez, and inland from Nice around Bellet.

When buying wines, look for these indications of quality: Vin de table is the lowest level of regulation; Vin de

Pays is produced from specified grapes in a specified region; and Vin à Appellation d'Origine Contrôlée (AOC) is the standard classification for wine with stringent regulations. The local AOC wine in the Riviera is Côtes de Provence. *The following are places where you can taste (dégustation) and buy wine: Le Château Sainte Roseline, 83460 Les Arcs-sur-Argens. Tel: 04 94 99 50 30. Excellent wine in a historic domaine. Maison des Vins de Bandol, Allées Vivien, 83150 Bandol. Tel: 04 94 29 45 03. Knowledgeable owner sells a range of Bandol wines. Château Gustinroux, 83570 Carcès. Tel: 04 94 04 52 51. Expansive vineyards once belonging to the Abbaye du Thoronet.*

Opposite: Olives and oil for sale in a local market
Above: A range of oil for tasting
Below: The *vendange*, or grape harvest, takes place in September

Corniche de l'Esterel

The terracotta volcanic rocks of the Esterel produce some of the most stunning landscapes on the Riviera. Rising to 618m (2,027ft), its hills are blanketed by *maquis*, a low growing scrub, interspersed with pine and cork oak. On the coast, wind and water have carved spectacular tufa columns and rocky coves. An excellent *corniche* highway hugs the littoral, offering spectacular views; but, to get to the heart of the Esterel, take to the excellent footpaths that criss-cross the region.

Fishing boats bobbing on the water

Fréjus

Set on an alluvial plain between the massifs of Maures and Esterel, Fréjus was established in Roman times as a staging post on the Via Aurelia, the main road from Rome to Gaul. The remains of Forum Julii are the most extensive in the Riviera.

The 2nd-century Arène (amphitheatre) is the most impressive building, with a capacity of 10,000. There is also a small Théâtre Romain at the heart of the city, now barely visible under ugly metal seating used for concerts. The Porte de Gaulles is the only remaining ancient gateway; the most complete section of wall is Butte St-Antoine, overlooking the old port.

The town's fine Musée Archéologique Municipal displays many artefacts found here and elsewhere along the coast, including the two-headed marble bust

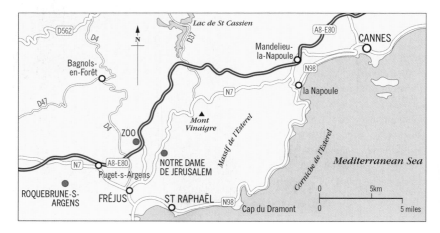

of Hermes (1st century), now a symbol of the town.

After the Romans left, it did not take long for the developers to move in. Fréjus became a bishopric and a 5th-century baptistery was erected, using recycled stone. Over the centuries, this developed into a large complex, now consisting of the Baptistery, a 12th-century two-storey *cloître* (cloister) and a monumental early-Gothic cathedral, with 15th-century frescoes featuring scenes from the Apocalypse and a fine 16th-century portal.

In the early 20th century, Fréjus became a military town. The Musée des Troupes de Marine (Museum of Navy Troops) tells the story of the Navy Corps from 1622 to the present day while Mémorial des Guerres en Indochine (Indo-China War Memorial) commemorates over 20,000 French soldiers who lost their lives in French Indochina. Amongst the legacies of the colonial troops who fought alongside the French are the Pagode Bouddhique Hông Hiên, a remarkable Buddhist pagoda built in 1917 by Vietnamese soldiers, and Mosquée de Missiri, a concrete replica of the Missiri de Djenné mosque in Mali, built by Senegalese soldiers stationed here in the 1920s (not possible to visit inside).

Arène, rue Henri Vadon, 83600 Fréjus. Tel: 04 94 51 34 31. Open: 1 Nov–31 Mar, Mon–Fri 10am–12pm, 1–5.30pm, Sat 9.30am–12pm, 1–5.30pm, Sun 8am–5pm; 1 Apr–31 Oct, Mon–Sat 10am–1pm, 2.30–6.30pm, Sun 9am–7pm. Closed: Tue & 1 Jan, 1 May and Christmas Day. Admission fee.
Théâtre Romain, rue du Théâtre Romain, 83600 Fréjus. Tel: 04 94 53 58 75. Open: 1 Nov–31 Mar, Mon–Fri 10am–12pm, 1–5.30pm, Sat 9.30am–12pm, 1–5.30pm, Sun 8am–5pm; 1 Apr–31 Oct, Mon–

The Arène at Fréjus is the largest Roman building on the Riviera

*Sat 10am–1pm, 2.30–6.30pm, Sun
9am–7pm. Closed: Tue & 1 Jan, 1 May
and Christmas Day. Admission fee.
Cloître de la Cathédrale de Fréjus, rue de
Fleury 58, 83600 Fréjus.
Tel: 04 94 51 26 31. Open: 15 Aug–11
May Tue–Sun 9am–12pm, 2–5pm, 12
May–14 Aug daily 9am–6.30pm. Free.
Musée Archéologique Municipal, place
Calvini, 83600 Fréjus. Tel: 04 94 52 15 78.
Open: 1 Nov–31 Mar, Mon–Fri
10am–12pm, 1.30–5.30pm, Sat
9.30am–12.30pm, 1.30–5.30pm;
1 Apr–31 Oct, Mon–Sat 10am–1pm,
2.30–6.30pm. Closed: Sun & 1 Jan,
1 May, Christmas Day. Admission fee.
Musée des Troupes de Marine, route des
Combattants d'Afrique du Nord, 83600
Fréjus. Tel: 04 94 40 81 75. Open:
15 June–14 Sept, 10am–12pm, 3–7pm;
15 Sept–14 Nov, 2–6pm; 15 Nov–14 Feb,
2–5pm; 15 Feb–14 June, 2–6pm. Closed:
Tue & Sat between 24 Dec and 2 Feb.
Free.
Mémorial des Guerres en Indochine, route
National 7, 83600 Fréjus.*

Roman remains dot the landscape around Fréjus

*Tel: 04 94 44 42 90. Open: 10am–5.30pm.
Closed Tue & 25 Dec–1 Jan, 5 Jan. Free.
Pagode Bouddhique Hông Hiên,
rue Henri Giraud 13, 83600 Fréjus.
Tel: 04 94 53 25 29. Open: 9am–12pm,
2–7pm. Free.*

Mont Vinaigre

Highest peak in the Massif de l'Esterel at
618m (2,027ft), it is only a 30-minute
walk from the car park through pine
woodland to the summit for a 360° view
over other Esterel peaks, including Pic
d'Ours and Pic du Cap Roux, Baie du
Fréjus and the Argens valley to the west.
It is rumoured that even the Alps are
visible on a clear day.

La Napoule

One of the finest purpose-built marinas
along the coast sealed la Napoule's
reputation amongst the yachting set.
The surrounding apartment blocks
give it a thoroughly modern feel, but
the vast fortified medieval château on
the waterfront hints at a longer
history.

The château was bought, restored and
augmented by American sculptor Henry
Clews and his architect wife as a family
home. Though it retains a medieval
cloister and Gothic dining room among
its original features, it has absorbed
other styles added by the Clews,
including Moorish elements. The tour
features the family's private rooms and
studio of the sculptor. Equally
impressive are the formal French
gardens and examples of Clews' pieces
on display.
*Château de La Napoule, 06210
Mandelieu-La Napoule. Tel: 04 93 49 95 05,*

www.chateau-lanapoule.com. Open: 7 Feb–7 Nov, 10am–6pm; 8 Nov– 6 Feb, Mon–Fri 2–6pm, Sat–Sun 10am–6pm. Admission fee.

Chapelle Notre Dame de Jérusalem

A work in progress when artist, writer, dramatist and film director Jean Cocteau died in 1963, this small chapel was completed according to his original design by Edouard Dermit in 1965. *Avenue Nicolaï, La Tour de Mare, 83600 Fréjus. Tel: 04 94 53 27 06. Open:*

1 Nov–31 Mar, Mon–Fri 1.30–5.30pm, Sat 9.30am–12.30pm, 1.30–5.30pm; 1 Apr–31 Oct, Mon–Fri 2.30–6.30pm, Sat 10am–1pm, 2–6.30pm. Closed: Tue and Sun, also 1 Jan, 1 May, Christmas Day. Free.

Parc Zoologique de Fréjus (Fréjus zoo)

Just 5km (3 miles) north of Fréjus, the zoo is a major tourist attraction established in 1971. The collection includes tigers, elephants and a variety

A long lunch is one of the pleasures of the Riviera

Rugged red rocks of the Esterel

of birds. It combines a safari park with a traditional zoo.

Parc Zoologique, Le Capitou, 83600 Fréjus. Tel: 04 98 11 37 37, www.zoo-frejus.com. Open: 1 June–30 Sept, 9.30am–6.30pm, 1 Oct–31 May, 10am–6pm. Admission fee.

Roquebrune-sur-Argens

Set dramatically in the shadow of the Rocher de Roquebrune, a red volcanic pillar rising to 383m (1,256ft), Roquebrune was founded in the 11th century. Scant remains of a stronghold can still be seen but the town centre features fine Renaissance architecture, particularly on rue Portiques. The 16th-century town church, Église St-Pierre-St-Paul, encompasses sub-chapels dating from the 1200s and 1400s with notable altarpieces.

This part of the Riviera has been settled far longer than that and the town's Archaeological Centre houses an interesting collection of finds, principally from the Bouverian caves (not open to the public), which were inhabited from 30,000 to 8,000 years ago.

There is an enjoyable walk above the village to Chapelle Notre-Dame-de Pitié with excellent views across the Fréjus plain.

Centre d'Exposition Archéologique Préhistoire et Histoire de Roquebrune,

Chapelle Saint-Jacques, Roquebrune.
Tel: 04 94 45 34 28. Open: June–Sept,
Tue–Sat 10am–12pm, 2–5.30pm;
Oct–May, Thur–Sat 10am–12pm, 2–6pm.
Closed: official hols. Admission charge.

Semaphore de Dramont

Isolated from the rest of the Massif de
l'Esterel by the coastal *corniche*, the Cap
de Dramont is an unspoilt spur of land
pointing out into the Mediterranean. A
30-minute walk leads to the Semaphore
de Dramont, an ancient signal point,
with views across the Golfe de Fréjus to
the Massif des Maures, or just offshore
to the Île d'Or. The paved path links
several secluded coastal inlets.

St Raphaël

St Raphaël began life during the Roman
era: this is where the upper echelons of
Fréjus society came for a little
relaxation. The popularity of the
modern resort is down to two men.
Alphonse Karr (1818–90), a journalist,
settled here in 1864 and invited his
Parisian friends – writers Dumas and de
Maupassant and the composer Berlioz
amongst them – to spend the winters
with him. The mayor, Félix Martin, had
an eye for an opportunity and used this
notoriety to redevelop St-Raphaël and
market it as the smartest resort on the
coast.

The 19th-century district around the
port remains intact, the best buildings
being Villa Roquerousse on promenade
René-Coty and Villa Paquerettes on
boulevard Félix Martin. The church of
Notre-Dame-de-la-Victoire-de-Lépante
in ornate neo-Byzantine style was built
in 1889.

The Casino was built on top of the
Roman resort, but many finds from the
site are on display in the Musée de
Préhistoire et d'Archéologique sous-
marine (Museum of Prehistory and
Underwater Archaeology) in the old
town, where you will also find the 12th-
century Église St-Pierre-des-Templiers,
built by the Templars as a chapel and
haven against pirate attack.
Musée de Préhistoire et d'Archéologique
sous-marine, place de la Vieille Église,
83705 Saint Raphaël. Tel: 04 94 19 25 75.
Open: 1 Oct–31 May, 10am–12pm,
2–5.30pm; 1 June–30 Sept, 10am–12pm,
3–6.30pm. Closed Fri and Mon.
Admission fee.

THE CICADA, SOUND OF THE RIVIERA

The rhythmic hum of the cicada is a
constant companion to your summer trip,
but the creature itself is a master of
camouflage, blending in perfectly with the
tree boughs that are its favourite habitat.

The insect spends 90 per cent of its life
underground in a larval stage; it emerges to
breed only when the temperature rises above
25°C (77°F) in the final short insect stage of its
life cycle. The choir you hear is male-voice only
– in fact the sound is a vibration of two plates
on the insect's abdomen – as he sets about his
task of wooing a mate.

Drive: The Massif de l'Esterel

This circular drive links the finest elements of the Esterel, from the Roman remains at Fréjus to rugged red rocks; from the sweeping views of the coastal *corniche* to the *maquis* (aromatic wild scrub) and pine forests of the hinterland. Many of these attractions demand you get your walking shoes on, or strip down to your swimming costume, but apart from the landscape these are half the attraction of the region.

Allow 4 hours.

1 Fréjus

Start your morning in Fréjus, exploring the numerous Roman remains, the expansive episcopal complex, the assorted war memorials and colonial temples.

Leave the town on the N98 coast road, boulevard d'Alger, which leads around the bay to Saint Raphaël via the Fréjus beaches.

2 Saint Raphaël

Though this too was a Roman town, the architecture of Saint-Raphaël offers a contrast to Fréjus: the late 19th-century district has some fine villas and the neo-Romanesque basilica is one of the finest modern churches along the Riviera.

Leave Saint Raphaël on the N98, the Route de la Corniche, through a series of small coastal settlements until you pass the car park for the walk to the Cap du Dramont on the right (5km or 3 miles).

3 Cap du Dramont

There is some exceptional coastal scenery here with footpaths out to the Semaphore, site of an old naval signal point. Being away from the road, this is the least busy section of coastline with several sheltered bays for sunbathing and swimming. The walk will take at least one hour out of your day.

Continue east along the coast road, the N98.

4 Corniche de l'Esterel

After the resort of Agay, development peters out and you enter the most spectacular section of the Corniche de l'Esterel. Seemingly endless sweeping bends offer tantalising glimpses of hidden coves with shimmering sands and azure waters. On the left there will be signposts to the Pic du Cap Roux and Pic d'Ours, both two-hour walks offering panoramic views.

Continue east on the N98 on through Théoule-sur-Mer. The route begins to become much more populated as you head into la Napoule.

5 la Napoule

The stunning medieval château of la Napoule, restored by American sculptor

Henry Clews, dominates the waterfront. In the background over 1,000 boats crowd the marina, regarded as one of the best new developments along the Riviera. *From la Napoule, head inland by following signs for Mandelieu. When you reach the N7, turn left – direction Fréjus – to start the inland section of the journey.*

6 Inland views

The N7 follows a verdant valley to the north of the Massif de l'Esterel, with sections of thick forest interspersed with low growing *maquis*. There are several footpaths leading into the heart of the mountains, the best being up to the peak of Mont Vinaigre for sublime distant views (car park after 17km, or 11 miles, from the last junction). Allow 90 minutes for the walk.

Continue along the N7 in the direction of Fréjus. After another 7km (4 miles) you will see a left turn to Notre Dame de Jérusalem.

7 Notre Dame de Jérusalem

The modern chapel, set in woodland, was designed and decorated by artist, novelist and film director Jean Cocteau, though it was completed after his death in 1963.

Continue to Fréjus on the N7 to complete the tour.

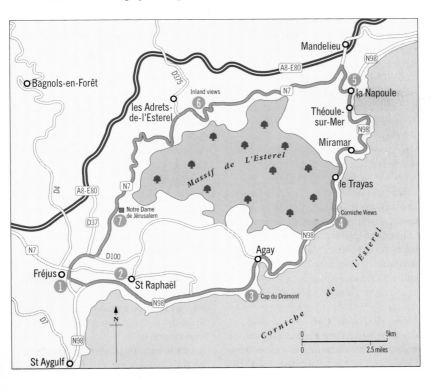

Cannes to Nice and Inland

Artists have flocked to this part of the Riviera for decades. Signac, Renoir and Picasso in their time found inspiration in the 'perfect light' that plays across the landscape.

The coastal resorts are the stuff of legend: Juan-les-Pins, Antibes and Cannes exude their own particular atmosphere. Inland, the silvery grey leaves of seemingly limitless olive trees shimmer in the breeze, interrupted only by the occasional medieval citadel, while unseen the power of water has eroded colossal caverns through the limestone underground.

The Carlton Hotel, a major landmark in Cannes

Antibes

One of the finest resort towns on the Riviera, Antibes sits on the western tip of the Baie des Anges, almost as a counterpoint to Nice to the east. It was the site of the Greek settlement Antipolis, but its modern reputation was made by the arrival of the wealthy American 'in crowd' in the 1920s. It is still one of the most fashionable harbours in the Mediterranean and cruising yachts flock to Port Vauban, also known as Billionaires' Wharf, to sit amongst the twin-screw, luxury vessels.

Casting a protective eye over the port is Fort Carré, built in 1550 but expanded by Vauban. The town's older castle, Château Grimaldi, with 12th- and 16th-century elements, became Picasso's studio in 1946 and the collection displayed here in Musée Picasso date from the period immediately following his arrival. Monumental works such as *La Joie de Vivre* are exhibited along with

a range of smaller canvases – many illustrating the inspiration the artist found along the coast here, in depictions of watermelon, fish and sea urchins.

Also featured is a series of works by Nicolas de Staël (1914–55), painted during the artist's period of residence just before his tragic suicide.

Antibes has an atmospheric old town just inland from the castle, in a set of narrow streets leading off Cours Massena, where the famed daily market is held under a wrought iron canopy. Église de l'Immaculée-Conception (Church of the Immaculate Conception) has 12th-century, Romanesque elements, though the western section dates from the 17th century. The Our Lady of the Rosary altarpiece (1515) with its painted miniatures is by Louis Bréa, the leading naïve painter of the Riviera.

The town's Musée Archéologique at Bastion St-André displays artefacts

covering 4,000 years of the region's history. Pride of place is taken by the reconstruction of a Roman ship complete with its cargo of amphorae.
Musée Picasso, Château Grimaldi. Tel: 04 92 90 54 20. Open: 1 Oct–31 May, 10am–12pm, 2–6pm; 1 June–30 Sept, 10am–6pm. Closed: Mon, 1 May, 1 Nov & 25 Dec. Admission fee.
Musée d'Archéologie, Bastion St-André. Tel: 04 93 34 00 39. Open: 1 Oct–31 May, 10am–12pm, 2–6pm; 1 June–30 Sept, 10am–6pm. Closed: 1 May, 1 Nov & 25 Dec. Admission fee.

'Souterroscope' or 'Grotte' de la Baume Obscure

Discovered in 1958, this underground labyrinth was all created by the power of water coursing through the rock over millions of years. Visitors can take a half-kilometre (550-yd) walk through the Galerie de la Course, 50m (165ft) below ground, to view cathedral-like caverns,

forests of stalactites and stalagmites and underground cascades and dams.
06460 Saint-Vallier de Thiey. Tel: 04 93 42 61 63. Open: Apr–June & Sept, Mon–Fri 10am–5pm, Sat–Sun 10am–7pm; July–Aug, daily 10am–7pm. Admission fee.

PABLO PICASSO (1881–1973)

'When I was a child, my mother said to me, "If you become a soldier, you'll be a general. If you become a monk, you'll end up Pope." Instead I became a painter and wound up as Picasso.'

Pre-eminent artist of the 20th century and arguably in the top ten of all time, Picasso was a child prodigy. He invented Cubism with his friend Georges Braque and pioneered *collage* and *essemblage* (the use of several materials on one piece) in sculpture. Born in Malaga, in Spain, he moved to Paris in 1904 and spent the latter years of his life on the Riviera.

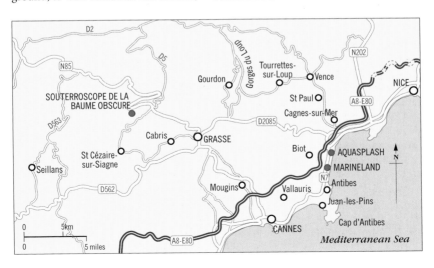

Picasso's studio in the Château Grimaldi, Antibes, is a major repository of his work

CAVES AND CAVERNS

Caverns the size of those at Baume Obscure and Saint-Cézaire (see p93) take millions of years to develop. Water drips through minuscule faults in the limestone rock, leaching a little limestone away with every drop. Over time the faults widen and the faults become caves then caverns.

At the same time, water dripping from the base of a fault leaves a little calcium behind. This builds up over millennia, creating a stalactite hanging from the ceiling. When water hits the floor of a cavern it leaves behind a little calcium that eventually builds up into a stalagmite, pointing upward toward the roof.

Biot

One of the most picturesque fortified villages in the Riviera, Biot is renowned for its crafts, since it produced amphorae and pottery for the Greeks and Romans. Biot glassware, produced since the 1950s, is found in bistros all along the coast.

The oldest part of the town comprises a tangle of medieval alleyways leading to the small central place des Arcades where the covered 16th-century walkways now offer shade to small cafés and restaurants. The town church has an altarpiece by Louis Bréa and an *Ecce Homo* (Christ wearing a crown of thorns) by Canavasio.

The artist Fernand Léger (1881–1955) is synonymous with Biot. He bought the Mas St André below the town to display his artistic legacy. The Musée National Fernand-Léger, designed by architect Andreï Svetchine, contains over 300 of his works, charting the development of his eclectic style, from which stem several 20th-century artistic genres.

Craft shops abound in the streets of the old town, or visit Verrerie de Biot where you can watch the vivid green and blue glassware being hand-blown.
Musée National Fernand-Léger, chemin du Val de Pome, 06410 Biot.
Tel: 04 92 91 50 31. Open: Oct–June,
10am–12pm, 2–5.20pm; July–Sept,
10am–12.30pm, 2–6pm. Closed: Tue
and 1 Jan, 1 May, Christmas Day.
Admission fee.

Cabris
Perched 550m (1,800ft) up, on the edge of the Provence Plateau, tiny Cabris is more famed for its excellent views than

its intrinsic character. The panorama to the south from the courtyard of the ruined 10th-century castle, place Mirabeau, takes in Mougins to the east, the Baie de la Napoule and the Lac de St-Cassien to the west. The village was totally rebuilt at the end of the 15th century, following an epidemic of the Black Death. Several narrow streets of sturdy stone houses sit atop the ancient terraced olive groves.

Cagnes-sur-Mer
The history of Cagnes-sur-Mer is inexorably tied up with the Grimaldi family, who in 1309 became lords of the town. They ruled from their fortified château until the Revolution. Attractions are concentrated in Haut-de-Cagnes lying in the shadow of the Grimaldi castle. The narrow alleys within are replete with fine Renaissance and

Fort Carré overlooks 'Billionaires' Wharf' in Antibes

17th-century mansions or *hôtels*, surrounded by medieval ramparts.

The forbidding walls of the castle give way to a dramatic Renaissance courtyard and its medieval rooms house the Château-Musée, a series of small collections, one illustrating the medieval history of Haut-de-Cagnes, another the cultivation of the olive tree. You'll also be able to enter the boudoir of the Marquise de Grimaldi, a suite of lavishly decorated rooms where the *trompe-l'oeil* on the ceiling of the oratory, *Fall of Phaeton* (1624), is perhaps the best on the Riviera. The rooms feature the artistic bequest of Suzy Solidor, 25 portraits of the famed *chanteuse* painted by 20th-century artistic luminaries such as Dufy, Lempicka and Cocteau.

The verdant hills that surround the town attracted the Impressionist artist Auguste Renoir (1841–1919), who spent the last 12 years of his life at the mansion of Les Collettes. The house is now the Musée Renoir, its rooms and the artist's studios preserved just as they were during his lifetime. A handful of Renoir's later canvases are also on display.

Château-Musée Grimaldi, place Grimaldi, 06800 Haut-de-Cagnes. Tel: 04 92 02 47 30. Open: summer, 10am–12pm, 2–6pm; winter, 10am–12pm, 2–7pm. Closed: Tue, 12 Nov–6 Dec and 1 Jan, 1 May, Christmas Day. Admission fee.
Musée Renoir, chemin des Collettes, 06800 Cagnes-sur-Mer. Tel: 04 93 20 61 07. Open: summer, 10am–12pm, 2–6pm; winter, 10am–12pm, 2–5pm. Closed: Tue, 1 Nov–21 Nov and 1 Jan, 1 May, Christmas Day. Admission fee.

Cannes

Home of the famed film festival, Cannes is the epitome of Riviera glitz and glamour, a town oozing success and confidence. The focus of modern Cannes is boulevard de la Croisette, the elegant promenade that runs the length of the wide sandy bay. You will find the in-crowd here, taking the sun on the private hotel beaches, gathering at chic beachfront restaurants, or shopping at the classy boutiques.

At the western end of the bay is the atmospheric old port, from where you can take ferry trips to the Îles des Lérins (*see p146*), and the Festival and

Biot is famed for its glassware

The expansive mature gardens of Renoir's house, now a museum

Conference Centre, which hosts the prize-giving ceremonies for the film festival. Here you will find the Allée des Étoiles (Pavement of the Stars), where the handprints of over 300 movie stars who have graced the Cannes red carpet are preserved in terracotta tiles.

Away from the razzmatazz is the oldest part of Cannes, a tiny district known as Le Suquet, which sits above the western end of the bay. Its quiet lanes, with some of the best bistros in town, lead ever upward to place de la Castre, dominated by 16th-century Notre Dame de l'Espérance for excellent

THE BIRTH OF CANNES

The modern reputation of Cannes was created by Lord Brougham, then British Chancellor of the Exchequer, who was on his way to Nice in 1834 until stopped by a cholera quarantine. He rested here, at what was then a small fishing village, and so captivated was he that he built a home here and continued to enjoy its mild winter climate for the next 34 years, extolling its virtues to a generation of English socialites who followed in his wake.

views of the Croisette and marina. The remains of the castle exhibit a worthwhile collection of archaeological artefacts from ancient Mediterranean civilisations, plus a collection of primitive African art, under the name of Musée de la Castre.

Musée de la Castre, Le Suquet, 06406 Cannes. Tel: 04 93 38 55 26. Open: June–Aug 10am–1pm, 3–7pm; Sept, 10am–1pm, 2–6pm; Oct–Mar, 10am–1pm, 2–5pm; Apr–May, 10am–1pm, 2–6pm. Closed: Mon and 1 Jan, 1 May, 1 Nov, 11 Nov, Christmas Day. Admission fee.

Cap d'Antibes

The small peninsula of Cap d'Antibes has some of the most sought-after real estate along the Riviera, with expansive private villas set amongst generous verdant gardens – though generally you can only catch a glimpse of these through locked gates as you pass. The Hotel Eden-Roc set in 8 hectares (20 acres) of grounds allows tourists to get closer to the Cap d'Antibes lifestyle, following in the footsteps of numerous artists, film stars and the occasional American army general.

For centuries pilgrims have flocked to Sanctuaire de la Garoupe to leave their votive offerings. The statue of Notre-Dame-de-Bon-Port, patron saint of sailors, is the focus of the procession in early July, when it travels back to the church from Antibes, carried by sailors. The Sebastopol icon, a splendid Russian-

The narrow streets of Le Suquet are home to many fine restaurants

The beach and boulevard de la Croisette in Cannes – a major playground for the 'jet set'

Orthodox work in Byzantine style dating from the 14th century, is also on display here.

Lovers of tropical plants should head to Jardin Thuret, a 4-hectare (10-acre) garden created by scientist Gustave Thuret in 1857 with over 3,000 rare and non-native species, from cactus to eucalyptus.

On the Juan-les-Pins coastline, visit Musée Napoléonien, housed in a military battery built by Napoléon. The collection charts his rise to power.

Sanctuaire de la Garoupe, place de la Garoupe, 06160 Antibes.

Tel: 04 93 67 36 01. Open: summer, 9.30am–12pm, 2.30–7pm; winter, 9.30am–12pm, 2.30–5pm. Free.
Jardin Thuret, boulevard du Cap, 06160 Antibes. Tel: 04 93 67 88 66. Open: summer, 8am–6pm, winter, 8am–5pm. Closed: Sat, Sun and 24 Dec–2 Jan. Free.
Musée Napoléonien, Batterie du Graillon, boulevard Kennedy, 06160 Juan-les-Pins. Tel: 04 93 61 45 32. Open Mon–Fri 9.15–11.45am, 2–5.45pm; Sat 9.15–11.45am. Closed Sat pm, Sun and Oct. Admission fee.

When Arnie Schwarzenegger in *Terminator 3* and Keanu Reeves in *The Matrix* both decided to dovetail the European launch of their films with the opening of the Cannes film festival, it brought this most French of gatherings to a world-wide audience.

While some welcomed the American acting A-Team, others lamented the 'Hollywoodisation' of what they considered an 'art-house' gathering – a celebration of the genre not of celebrity. Yet over the last decade the status of the festival has been raised to new, some would say, stellar heights.

The festival was established in 1939 and funded by the French government. They chose Cannes for its mild climate and its hours of sunshine. The inaugural festival had to be cancelled because of the outbreak of war – not a very auspicious start.

The first festival was held in September 1946 (it moved to April in 1950, then to May in 1957) with mainly avant-garde productions that pushed the boundaries of cinema, with a particular strength in French and other non-English-language films.

For the fans and the media, the glamorous parties attended by stars and starlets are the focus of attention. The nearest that most movie fans get to a screening is standing on the pavement outside. But this is really a festival for

1997 LE GOÛT DE LA CERISE · 1998 L'ÉTERNITÉ ET UN JOUR · 1999 ROSETTA · 2000 DANCER IN THE DARK · LA CHAMBRE DU FILS

1993 ADIEU MA CONCUBINE · 1994 PULP FICTION · 1995 UNDERGROUND 1996 SECRETS ET MENSONGES · L'ANGUILLE

MENSONGES ET VIDÉO · 1990 SAILOR ET LULA · 1991 BARTON FINK · 1992 LES MEILLEURES INTENTIONS · LA LEÇON DE PIANO

1985 PAPA EST EN VOYAGE D'AFFAIRES · 1986 THE MISSION · 1987 SOUS LE SOLEIL DE SATAN · 1988 PELLE LE CONQUÉRANT

1981 L'HOMME DE FER · 1982 MISSING · 1982 YOL · NARAYAMA · 1984

1978 L'ARBRE AUX SABOTS · 1979 LE TAMBOUR · 1979 APOCALYPSE NOW · 1980 KAGEMUSHA · 1980

the film industry, not for cinema-goers. And this is borne out by the amount of wheeler-dealing that goes on behind the scenes. This major marketplace for the film industry brings together budding writers and directors with prospective producers – the ones who wield the cash. It is the place to make your sales pitch and get projects off the ground. All this goes on behind closed doors or at the lavish parties – something for which there is not really a platform in Hollywood.

Several prizes are on offer during the ten-day festival, including one for non-mainstream film and also a critic's choice, but the main interest is in the prize for best film – the famed *Palme d'Or*, awarded by an annual panel of guests including actors and celebrities. Over the years films from 21 countries, including South Africa, Brazil, Turkey and more than one from Japan, have won the prize. The panels have also recognised ground-breaking genres, such as the 1956 winner *Le Monde du Silence* by Jacques Cousteau and Louis Malle, which was the first feature film shot underwater.

Though many films will not stick in the mind of English-speaking mainstream movie-goers, here is a selection of some international *Palme d'Or* winners that you may well recognise.

1949 *The Third Man*, Carol Reed
1970 *M*A*S*H*, Robert Altman
1976 *Taxi Driver*, Martin Scorsese
1979 *Apocalypse Now*,
       Francis Ford Coppola
1984 *Paris, Texas*, Wim Wenders
1986 *The Mission*, Roland Joffé
1989 *Sex, Lies and Videotape*,
       Steven Soderbergh
1993 *The Piano*, Jane Campion
1994 *Pulp Fiction*, Quentin Tarentino
1996 *Secrets and Lies*, Mike Leigh
2002 *The Pianist*, Roman Polanski
2003 *Elephant*, Gus Van Sant

Opposite, above: Joan Collins' handprints set in terracotta on Allée des Etoiles
Opposite, below: Previous *Palme d'Or* winners commemorated in bronze
Above: The ultra-modern Palais des Festivals hosts the *Palme d'Or* awards ceremony

Le Puy is the oldest quarter of Grasse

Gorges du Loup

Nature at its most dramatic is on display at the Gorges du Loup. The power of ice and water has eroded a vertical path through the schist mountains around Grasse, where the River Loup continues to whittle away at the rocky river bed. Along the route, stop at the Cascade de Courmes, a 40-m (130-ft) water-chute, the Saut du Loup a gigantic eroded bowl, and the Cascade des Demoiselles where the surrounding vegetation has been petrified by the limestone carried in the spray from the river.

The D3 travels high above the western flank, offering exceptional overviews of the gorge and the hundreds of hectares of oak forest that blanket the area, with long views south to the Mediterranean coast.

Gourdon

Perched on a rocky spur some 500m (1,600ft) above the Gorges de Loup, the medieval hamlet of Gourdon was in steep decline in the middle of the 20th century, but has been transformed with the arrival of craft shops, restaurants and cafés. Most people make their way to the church square for the amazing panorama, said to be up to 50km (30 miles) on a clear day.

The town's Saracen château, built in the 13th century with Renaissance additions, was restored in the 17th century. It houses a collection of antique arms, the Musée de Peinture Naïve (Museum of Naïve Painting), a small but high-quality collection dating from the 1920s to the 1970s and an exceptional collection of Art Deco rooms designed by visionaries of the style. The formal gardens designed by Le Nôtre, set on a series of massive medieval arches, are outstanding.

Château de Gourdon, place du Château, 06620 Gourdon. Tel: 04 93 09 68 02. Open: 1 June–30 Sept, 11am–1pm, 2–7pm; 1 Oct–31 May, 2–6pm. Closed Tue. Admission fee.

Grasse

Regarded as the world capital of perfume, Grasse is surrounded by the flower fields that have produced its raw materials since the 16th century. The town trades on its 'fragrant' reputation, but has lost much of the charm that brought Queen Victoria here in the later 19th century, its quiet corners given over to graffiti and litter. However it has some important collections to enjoy.

Head to the Musée International de la Parfumerie to discover the history of perfume production, both here and around the world. Three commercial perfumiers still operate in the city: Fragonard, Galimard and Molinard each have a small museum and guided tour. Fragonard and Molinard also have tours of their flower gardens during the spring and early summer when the blooms are harvested.

The town's favourite son is artist Jean-Honoré Fragonard (1732–1806). Villa-Musée Fragonard, the mansion where he

You can sample a range of fragrances on a perfumery tour

When Catherine de Medici (1519–89), Queen of France, initiated a new fashion for perfumed gloves, she and the whole French upper class headed to the 'leather city' of Grasse to be kitted out. From these small beginnings the cathedral city developed into the world's capital of perfume.

Grasse

This city had been producing gloves and gauntlets for centuries, and also exported finished skins. Tanners used perfumes in a basic way to try and freshen the air during the very smelly leather-treatment process. The city was in an excellent position to take advantage of the commercial opportunity the queen brought, with a climate perfect for flower production during spring and early summer.

Ironically, in the following centuries, the leather industry in Grasse fell into decline but the demand for perfume increased, as hygiene improved and both men and women longed to smell fresh and sweet. The industry became more organised in the 19th century, with factories being opened – the first by Molinard in 1849, followed by Galimard and then the youngest, Fragonard, in 1926, named after Grasse's most famous son, the painter Jean-Honoré Fragonard.

All the perfume houses in Grasse still sell finished fragrances under their own brand names (the signature fragrance produced by Fragonard has its own faithful following), but the main earning potential is in supplying raw essences, the 'building blocks' of a fragrance, to other perfume and cosmetics houses.

Making perfumes

Although the perfume can be removed from flower petals through distillation (flowers are boiled in water, then the

each will bring, to make the overall finished smell. The skilled blender is called a *nez* ('nose'), after the most important tool of their trade. There are only a handful of these 'masters of the art' in the world and they command a high salary.

You can visit the following perfumeries in Grasse:

Fragonard, boulevard Fragonard 20. Tel: 04 93 36 44 65. (Flower fields at les 4 Chimins, route de Cannes. Tel: 04 93 77 94 30.)

Molinard, boulevard Victor Hugo 60. Tel: 04 92 42 33 11.

Galimard, route de Pégomas. Tel: 04 93 09 20 00.

resulting 'essence' is condensed) or by *enflourage* (where petals are pressed into animal fat, and then washed with alcohol), today's are produced through a process of extraction. The flower petals are mixed with a solvent which, when it evaporates, leaves behind *concrète* or a concretion of 40 per cent perfume and 60 per cent wax. When the wax is removed (using alcohol), what remains is the purest perfume essence possible. It takes 1 tonne of petals to produce 3kg (7lb) of *concrète*.

Though this in itself is an amazing process, these 'essential' perfumes are only the starting point for the finished product. They must be diluted, then blended, and each new finished fragrance needs a 'recipe' so that it can be produced in commercial quantities. The blending of the fragrances is a highly skilled job. It takes years of training and a natural flair to understand exactly which 'top notes', 'middle notes' and 'base notes' will blend together, and the exact qualities

Opposite: The basic raw material of every *bouquet*
Above: A *nez* at work
Below: Eye-catching displays of packaged fragrances

spent his years during the Revolution, displays a selection of his works, but the ground-floor panels depicting *The Pursuit of Love*, commissioned by the Duchesse du Barry in 1771 and which she subsequently refused to accept, are copies; the originals now hang in New York.

Le Puy, old Grasse, was an episcopal city and boasts numerous Renaissance palaces and mansions. The high nave of the Cathédrale Notre-Dame-du-Puy is the earliest example of Gothic religious architecture in the region. There are several paintings of interest in the interior. Fragonard painted few religious scenes, but his *Washing of the Feet* hangs here. There is a triptych attributed to Bréa and three works by Peter-Paul Rubens (1577–1640) – *Crucifixion*, *The Crown of Thorns* and *St Helen in Exaltation of the Holy Cross*.

The 18th-century mansion 'Petit Trianon', with some exceptional Louis XIV decoration, houses the Musée d'Art et d'Histoire de Provence (Museum of Provençal Art and History) which is the Riviera's premier heritage collection, encompassing traditional costumes and furniture, *santons*, ceramics from Biot, Vallauris and Moustiers, paintings by Provençal artists and a collection of archaeological finds from the region.
Musée d'Art et d'Histoire de Provence, rue Mirabeau 2, 06130 Grasse.
Tel: 04 93 36 01 61. Open: June–Sept, 10am–7pm, Oct–May, 10am–12.30pm, 2–5.30pm. Closed Tue and official holidays. Admission fee.
Musée International de la Perfumerie, place du Cours Honoré Cresp, 06130 Grasse. Tel: 04 93 36 80 20. Open: June–Sept, 10am–7pm, Oct–May, 10am–12.30pm, 2–5.30pm. Closed: Tue and official holidays. Admission fee.
Villa-Musée Fragonard, Boulevard

Gourdon commands superb views from its rocky precipice

Craft shops are a feature of all hilltop villages

Fragonard 23, 06130 Grasse.
Tel: 04 93 36 01 61. Open: June–Sept,
10am–7pm, Oct–May, 10am–12.30pm,
2–5.30pm. Closed: Tue and official
holidays. Admission fee.

Juan-les-Pins

One of the longest established of the
Riviera resorts, Juan-les-Pins became
ultra-fashionable in the 1920s amongst
the American *nouveau riche*. It is still an
attractive site, with a fine sand beach
2km (1¼ miles) long, backed by the
popular Promenade du Soleil – where
the wealthy come to take their evening
stroll. Perhaps slightly more staid than

THE ROUTE DE NAPOLÉON

When Napoléon curtailed his short-lived
first exile on the island of Elba, he set
foot once again on metropolitan France at
Golfe-Juan on 1 March 1815. After spending
the night in Cannes, he sought to speed his
way north to Paris by avoiding towns and
cities he knew to have anti-Bonaparte
sentiments. Passing by way of Grasse, the tiny
entourage took donkey tracks via St-Vallier,
Escragnolles and Séranon before passing
through Sisteron and on to Grenoble. You
can follow in the emperor's footsteps on
the 'Route de Napoléon'.

Antibes and Cannes, it is nevertheless famed for its International Jazz Festival, which has been inviting the cream of talent since the 1950s.

Marineland

The largest complex of family attractions along the coast lies just east of Antibes, where Marineland has an excellent collection including killer whales, dolphins, sea lions, seals and penguins, plus the expected shark tunnel and spectacular shows.

Next door, Jungle de Papillons (Butterfly Jungle) plays host to species from across the world plus a collection of giant 'creepy-crawlies' and crocodiles, whilst across the street you will find Antibesland, an old-fashioned funfair. All this is enough to keep kids of all ages happy for at least a couple of days. *Marineland, off RN7, La Brague, Antibes. Tel: 04 93 33 49 49, www.marineland.fr Open: 10am–9pm. July–Aug. Check website for full details. Admission fee.*

Mougins

This typical medieval Provençal village caught the eye of Pablo Picasso and it was here that he spent his last days (1961–73) in a *mas* (traditional stone farmhouse) called L'Antre du Minotaure (Lair of the Minotaur). You will find some of the artist's private moments

Small fishing boats bobbing in the harbour at Juan-les-Pins

captured in the permanent collection of the Musée de la Photographie.

The circular medieval village sits within the remnants of a 12th-century curtain wall, its tangle of narrow lanes replete with old stone cottages set around place de la Mairie with its shady elm tree. At every corner, artists carry on Picasso's rich legacy.

Musée de la Photographie, porte Sarrazine, 06250 Mougins. Tel: 04 93 75 85 67. Open: July–Sept, daily 10am–8pm; Oct–June, Wed–Sat 10am–12pm, 2–6pm, Sun 2–8pm. Admission fee.

Seillans

Typical of many Provençal perched villages, though rather more workaday than most, Seillans is a maze of cobbled alleyways and small squares decorated with fountains. The settlement took its present form in the 11th century when monks of the order of Saint-Victor built a fortified cloister here. A small 11th-century château, now a private home, the 12th-century Mairie (Town Hall) and the town church of Saint-Léger now form the heart of the community.

The Surrealist artist Max Ernst (1891–1976) settled in Seillans during the last days of his life. In the 1990s, his wife Dorothy Tanning bequeathed almost 70 of his works to the village; they are now displayed in The Tanning Donation – Ernst Collection.

The Tanning Donation, Max Ernst Collection, rue de l'Église, 83440 Seillans. Tel: 04 94 76 85 91. Open: May–Sept, daily 10am–12.30pm, 2–6pm; Oct–Apr, Mon–Fri 10am–12.30pm, 2–5pm, Sat 2–5pm. Admission fee.

St-Cézaire-sur-Siagne

The houses of St-Cézaire cascade over the lip of the Siagne Valley with dramatic views 300m (1,000ft) down to the river gorge. In Roman times the area was a market garden for the coastal towns – in fact, the Romanesque chapel in the village displays a Gallo-Roman sarcophagus – but the heart of the present village is medieval, fortified by the counts of Provence in the 16th century.

West of the village lie the Grottes de St-Cézaire (Caves of St-Cézaire), a series of interconnected limestone caverns over 200m (660ft) long and 40m (130ft) below ground, with exceptional rock formations, stalagmites and stalactites.

Grottes de Saint Cézaire, boulevard du Puit d'Amon, 06780 Saint-Cézaire sur Siagne. Tel: 04 93 60 22 35, www.lesgrottesdesaintcezaire.fr. Open: 15 Feb–31 Mar & Oct, daily 2.30–5pm; Apr–May, daily 2.30–5.30pm; June & Sept, daily 10.30am–12pm, 2.30–6pm; July–Aug, daily 10.30am–6.30pm; Nov–14 Feb, Sun 2.30–5pm. Admission fee.

St Paul (de Vence)

Beloved of artists in the early 20th century and to supermodels and film stars in the early 21st, St Paul is the most celebrated of the medieval villages that dot the hinterland of the Riviera. It is still an active artists' community, but most of the Renaissance houses have been given over to upmarket galleries, shops and restaurants giving the village more the atmosphere of a themed shopping mall than a living community. Auberge de la Colombe d'Or, the once humble café where the artists like Picasso and Modigliani socialised, has been transformed into one of the most renowned eateries in the Riviera.

The village is set inside splendid medieval ramparts pierced by Port de Vence (Vence Gate). Rue Grand has been the main street since Roman times and is flanked by splendid, arcaded 17th-century mansions and graced by the Grand Fountain (1850).

In place de l'Église at the top of the town, St Paul – the Gothic collegiate church founded in the 12th century – contains a dramatic painting of

St Catherine attributed to Tintoretto. A small town museum combines wax medieval figures and photographs to give a historical overview of the village. The only part of the medieval castle that remains is the *donjon* (keep), which dominates the square.

Fondation Maeght is one of the world's most important art museums, offering a unique compendium of modern painting, sculpture and ceramics. Launched by the donation of works by Aimé and Marguerite Maeght in 1964, it now comprises 6,000 pieces, with works by Braque, Chagall, Léger,

A *promenade* along the seafront in Juan-les-Pins

Medieval cobbled street in Seillans

THE ARTISTS OF ST PAUL DE VENCE

The dust of time hung heavily over St Paul when it was 'discovered' by the artistic set during the early 1920s. Signac and Modigliani led the way, hanging out in the local café and paying their bills with recently completed canvases when funds were low. When Picasso and Chagall arrived in their wake, the barter system was well established and over time the café (now the Auberge de Colombe d'Or) became one of Europe's richest depositories of 20th-century art and a magnet for today's jet set.

Kandinsky and Miró. The building and grounds, designed by Joseph-Louis Sert, were designed to incorporate artworks including a population of 'skinny' people, life-size bronzes by Alberto Giacometti in the courtyard. In summer, when the museum hosts avant-garde temporary exhibitions, the permanent collections are not on show.
Fondation Maeght, 06570 St-Paul. Tel: 04 93 32 81 63, www.fondation-maeght.com Open: 1 July–30 Sept, 10am–7pm; 1 Oct– 30 June, 10am–12.30pm, 2.30–6pm. Admission fee.

Tourettes-sur-Loup

This village of arts and crafts has a strength in weaving, and many of the 16th- and 17th-century houses within the ramparts of Tourettes have been converted into workshops and galleries, but this has not taken too much of the raw character away. Narrow, cobbled Grand'rue offers a circular tour through the heart of the old town. St-Grégoire church contains a pagan Gallo-Roman altar dedicated to Mercury whilst Chapelle St-Jean is decorated with modern frescoes by Ralph Souplaut, completed in 1959.

Tourettes is the capital of violet country and the surrounding fields are heady with scent and brilliant with colour between November and March.

Vallauris

Picasso reinvigorated the dying craft of pottery in Vallauris and it is now the leading industry of the town. The major legacy of the artist is Musée National Picasso la Guerre et la Paix, centring on two contrasting epic murals – *La Guerre* ('War') and *La Paix* ('Peace') – commissioned by the town for a deconsecrated Romanesque chapel. *Musée National Picasso la Guerre et la Paix, Château Musée de Vallauris, place de la Liberation, 06220 Vallauris. Tel: 04 93 64 16 05. Open: June–Sept, 10am–6.30pm; Oct–May, 10am–12pm, 2–6pm. Closed Tue. Admission fee.*

Vence

A circular old town of some character and lineage lies at the heart of Vence's sprawling suburbs. An early bishopric, the cathedral was founded in the 4th century on the site of a Roman temple (look for Roman inscriptions on some of the reused stone in the façade) and later rebuilt in Romanesque style. The baptistery displays *Moses in the Bullrushes*, a mosaic by Chagall.

Matisse considered Chapelle du Rosaire (Chapel of the Rosary, also known as Chapelle Matisse) his masterpiece. He designed the interior during renovations in the late 1940s. Monochrome exterior walls are topped by a mosaic of polychrome tiles, whilst the stark interior has murals representing the Stations of the Cross.

The 17th-century Château de Villeneuve, town castle of the barons de Villeneuve, houses the gallery of Fondation Émile Hugues, showing works of Matisse, Dufy and Chagall amongst others, and the inspiration they derived from the area.

Chapel du Rosaire, avenue Henri Matisse 46, 06140 Vence. Tel: 04 93 58 03 26. Open: Mon, Wed, Sat 2–5.30pm; Tue, Thur 10–11.30am, 2–5.30pm. Closed: Fri (except during French school hols, when open 2–5.30pm), 15 Nov–15 Dec. Free.

Château de Villeneuve (Fondation Émile Hugues), place du Frêne, 06140 Vence. Tel: 04 93 24 24 23. Open: summer, 10am–6pm; winter, 10am–12.30pm, 2–6pm. Closed Tue. Admission fee.

Matisse's Vence masterpiece, *la Chapelle du Rosaire*, is a *tour de force* of Minimalism

Drive: The Cap d'Antibes

This drive around the Cap d'Antibes, from Antibes to Juan-les-Pins, takes in a series of disparate attractions. Just as important are the wealth of fine private villas you will pass on your journey; real estate that confirms the reputation of Cap d'Antibes as one of the most upmarket locations on the Riviera.

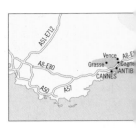

1 Antibes

Begin at Antibes, leaving the car and exploring the town. You can browse at the market on Cours Masséna, visit the large marina just beyond the last remaining section of town wall, enjoy the Roman artefacts in the Archaeological Museum and of course enjoy the artworks at the Picasso Museum.

Leave the town southwards via boulevard Maréchal Leclerc, and keep the coastline on your left as you move into Boulevard James Wyllie. You will pass the beaches of Plage du Ponteil and Plage de la Salis. Turn right away from the coast at

Old Antibes, nestled within its remaining 'curtain' walls

boulevard Gardiole Bacon. You will take a right at avenue Aimé Bourreau and sharp right at route du Phare, to reach Chapelle de la Garoupe.

2 Chapelle de la Garoupe

This is the most important pilgrimage site on the Cap d'Antibes. It holds the statue of Notre-Dame-de-Bon-Port, revered by sailors, and a 14th-century Russian icon brought back to France after the siege of Sebastapol. The Phare de la Garoupe (Garoupe lighthouse) also stands on the site.

Return down route du Phare and continue ahead the short distance southwest on avenue Malespine until you reach the crossroads. Turn left on to boulevard Francis Meilland, then a right at boulevard John Fitzgerald Kennedy. Look out for the turning into the drive of the Hotel Eden Roc on the left.

3 Eden Roc Hotel

Set in 8 hectares (20 acres), the Eden Roc is a sumptuous Edwardian villa that has welcomed the rich and famous since it opened its doors in 1914.

Return to boulevard John Fitzgerald Kennedy and just 200m (182ft) further along is Musée Napoléonien.

The genteel Hotel Eden Roc once welcomed General Eisenhower

4 Musée Napoléonien

This 18th-century bastion was built under Napoléon's orders and has papers, charts and other artefacts relating to the emperor's career. From the bastion there are views across the Golfe Juan to Juan-les-Pins. Napoléon landed here after he escaped his first exile on the Mediterranean island of Elba.

From the museum follow the coast road northwards, along boulevard du Maréchal Juin, past several beaches. At Chemin du Tamisier take a right, heading inland, then right again at Chemin Raymond, where you will find the Jardin Thuret.

5 Jardin Thuret

This 4-hectare (10-acre) exotic garden is named after its creator Gustave Thuret, who attempted to acclimatise tropical species here. You can stroll amongst 3,000 different species.

Return to the coast and pick up boulevard du Maréchal Juin once again, taking a right into Juan-les-Pins.

6 Juan-les-Pins

Sitting at the western head of the Cap d'Antibes as a counterpart to Antibes on the east, Juan-les-Pins does not have the long history of its neighbour, being very much a 19th- and 20th-century settlement. Enjoy the seafront promenade where you can take refreshment while watching the world go by.

Nice

Grande Dame of the Riviera, Nice is its 'capital'. A cosmopolitan metropolis of 400,000, it combines thriving industrial city, holiday resort and focal point of art culture and history, in addition to being the main entry point by air and sea. Nice didn't officially become part of France until 1860, having belonged to the Count du Savoy from the 14th century. It still has its own regional dialect and a certain 'Latin' *je ne sais quoi*.

Beach umbrellas provide welcome shade

Nice presents many different faces. Old Nice has narrow streets of pastel mansions interspersed by elegant squares, while the 18th- and 19th-century city is characterised by wide boulevards flanked by Republic mansions (built during the mid-18th century), punctuated by a rash of striking modern buildings. Around the port, tall tenements once housed the stevedores and fishermen, while the inland suburb of Cimiez offers the most refined villas in the city.

It was the mild microclimate that first drew tourists but the coming of the railway really increased its popularity. Even Queen Victoria came to take the air, resulting in a rush of the British upper classes.

Cathédrale Orthodoxe Russe St-Nicolas

Symbol of the close connection between the old Russian aristocracy and the French Riviera, the cathedral is the largest Russian Orthodox place of worship outside the motherland.

Built using the finest materials, following generous donations by members of the Russian royal family, the cathedral was completed in 1912, but it benefited from several valuable ecclesiastical donations after the Russian Revolution in 1917.

The exterior's gilded domes lend an exotic air to the city skyline, but the opulent interior is the highlight; a wealth of frescoes and gold leaf. The iconostasis is an artistic *tour de force*, combining religious art from two Moscow churches, Jaroslav and St Basil the Blessed.

Boulevard Tzarevitch, 06000 Nice. Open: Mon–Sat 10am–12.30pm, 2–6pm; Sun 2–6pm. Closest bus 71, 75, 7, 15 with 200m (220 yds) walk. Admission fee.

Cathédrale Ste-Réparate

Nice's primary church is dedicated to the city's patron, who was martyred in Asia Minor. Completed in 1650 in Baroque style, the interior is a sumptuous *embarras de richesses* of ornate plasterwork.

Place Rosetti, 06000 Nice. Open: daily, Mon–Fri 9am–12pm, 3–6pm; Sun 3–6pm. Free.

RUSSIAN ARISTOCRACY IN THE RIVIERA

Though the British 'discovered' the Riviera, they were joined with equal enthusiasm by the Russian aristocracy, who were pleased to escape the bitter Russian winters for the temperate Mediterranean. They used their considerable wealth to construct impressive villas and two Russian Orthodox basilicas, in Nice and Cannes.

The Bolshevik revolution in 1917 brought a sudden end to this carefree existence. Russian nobility was obsolete. Many died while survivors in exile were impoverished by the loss of their lands.

The Orthodox basilicas of the Riviera benefited from the Russian Revolution, receiving a cache of priceless holy relics dispatched from Moscow to keep them out of the hands of the atheist revolutionaries.

The Negresco hotel – *belle époque* architecture at its best

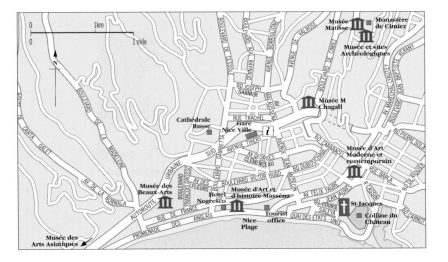

Colline du Château (Castle Hill)

This 92m (302ft) hill lying west of the port offers panoramic views across the old city and along the Baie des Anges. The location of the city fort until it was destroyed in 1706 (hence the name), it also has Greek and Roman remains indicating its strategic importance. Although you can take a lift to the summit, it is a pleasure to walk through the woodland. It also makes the perfect picnic site after your explorations.
On the coast between the old town and the port. Open: dawn–dusk. Free.

Cours Saleya

The social centre of Old Nice, Cours Saleya is one of the most complete *boulevards* on the Riviera, flanked by pastel buildings including the Caïs de Pierla Palace where Picasso spent much of the 1920s and 1930s garnering inspiration for his stunning canvases. The façades of the Chapelle de la Miséricorde – a magnificent Baroque design from 1740 – and Église St-François-de-Paule add drama to the whole ensemble. Cours Saleya hosts Nice's atmospheric flower and vegetable market.
Flower market, Cours Saleya. Open: Tue–Sat 6am–5.30pm, Sun 6am–12pm. Monday is an antique market.

Monastère Franciscain (Franciscan Monastery)

Founded by the Benedictines in the 9th century, the convent was taken over by the Franciscans in the 16th century. The highlight of the complex is the main church, Église Notre-Dame-de-l'Assomption, with paintings by Louis Bréa, the leading artist of the Nice Primitive School, and a combined Renaissance/Baroque altarpiece. The small museum, in a restored section of the buildings, displays other works of art along with documents and a restored friar's room *c.* 1700.
Place du Monastère, 06000 Nice. Tel: 04 93 81 00 04. Open: Mon–Sat 10am–12pm, 3–6pm. Closed: religious holidays. Bus nos 15, 17, 20, 22. Free.

Musée d'Art Moderne et d'Art Contemporain (Museum of Modern and Contemporary Art)

At the forefront of the development of art since the 1960s, Nice now has an impressive vehicle for its legacy – a fine building designed by Yves Bayard and Henri Vidal.

A room with a view in old Nice

French Nouveau Réalisme paralleled American Pop Art in its use of modern consumables. A large area of gallery space is devoted to Yves Klein, a founder of the movement, whose use of a certain shade of blue led to it being named International Klein Blue (IKB).

The museum has fine examples of international modern art, including works by Karen Appel (a member of the COBRA movement) and Andy Warhol (doyen of American Pop), but devotes the greatest attention to the Nice School, a group of artists who have developed through and contributed to movements in modern art in the last 30 years.
Promenade des Arts, 06000 Nice. Tel: 04 93 62 61 62. Open: Tue–Sun 10am–6pm. Closed: 1 Jan, Easter Sun, 25 Dec. Bus nos 1, 2, 3, 4, 5, 6, 7, 9, 10, 14, 16A, 17, 25. Admission fee.

Musée des Arts Asiatiques (Museum of Asiatic Arts)

Devoted to art from across Asia, the museum is housed in a stunning building designed around Asian philosophical and religious doctrines by Japanese architect Kenzo Tange.

Each gallery is devoted to a particular civilisation, from China and Japan to Cambodia and India, featuring exquisite objects used in religious worship and domestic rituals. There is also a Japanese tea-room where you can experience the genuine tea ceremony.
405 promenade des Anglais, 06000 Nice. Tel: 04 92 29 37 00, www.arts-asiatiques.com. Open: Wed–Mon: 1 May–15 Oct, 10am–6pm, 16 Oct–30 Apr, 10am–5pm. Closed 1 Jan, 1 May, Christmas Day. Bus nos 9, 10, 23. Admission fee.

Musée des Beaux-Arts Jules-Chéret (Jules-Chéret Fine Arts Museum)

Assembled around a donation of works by Emperor Napoléon III in 1860, and housed in an 1870s' mansion built for a Ukrainian princess, this museum has one of the finest collections of fine art in France. Works date from the 15th to the 20th century, with major strengths including the 17th-century Italian school, local artistic dynasty the Van Loo family, and 18th-century French and Italian Impressionists and

Shopping for fresh produce in the market on Cours Saleya

post-Impressionists, with examples by Degas, Monet, Sisley, Boudin and (sculptures by) Rodin.

33 avenue des Baumettes, 06000 Nice. Tel: 04 92 15 28 28. Open: Tue–Sun 10am–6pm. Bus nos 3, 5, 7, 8, 9, 10, 11, 11B, 12, 14, 22, 24, 38, 60, 62. Admission fee.

Musée Matisse

A showcase of works by the leading exponent of Fauvism, Henri Matisse (1869–1954), charts both the development of his style and the ease with which he moved between genres. Housed in a 17th-century villa with a remarkable modern extension, paintings range from *Still Life, Books*, painted in 1890, to *Flowers and Fruit*, his last work, as well as over 250 preparatory drawings and sketches, 50 bronze sculptures, silk-screen prints and a monumental tapestry, *Polynesia*. The whole collection was given to the city by the artist himself in 1953.

164 avenue des Arènes, 06000 Nice. Open: Wed–Mon 10am–6pm. Bus nos 15, 17, 20, 22, 25. Admission fee.

Musée National Message Biblique Marc Chagall (Marc Chagall Biblical Message Museum)

A dramatic modern gallery designed by A Harmant and opened in 1972, this museum dedicated to Marc Chagall (1887–1985) houses his own donations to the city and the world's most important collection of his work.

The 17 canvases that make up 'Biblical Message' were painted between 1954 and 1967 and depict the painter's own interpretation of the Bible's story.

Highlights include the evocative interpretations of the *Creation of Man* and *Garden of Eden*. Other rooms display the 39 gouaches, 105 etchings and copper plates, and 200 sketches that the artist used in his build-up to the finished pieces.

Avenue Dr Ménard, 06000 Nice. Tel: 04 93 53 87 20, www.musee-chagall.fr. Open: Wed–Mon: July–Sept, 10am–6pm; Oct–June, 10am–5pm. Closed: some bank holidays. Admission fee.

Promenade des Anglais

This long, wide seafront promenade parallels the Baie des Anges (Bay of the Angels) from central Nice west towards Antibes. The elegant palm-lined walkway with its gardens, smart squares and splendid mansions still symbolises the Riviera for many. The most renowned building is the Negresco hotel, a *belle époque* confection built at the turn of the 20th century. You will find the whole of Nice comes out to stroll along the seafront during the day or early evening.

The promenade gets its name because in the early 1800s the Reverend Lewis Way donated money to build a coastal footpath as a way to allow easy access to the beach for the growing English ex-patriot community in the city. When the road was built, the name promenade des Anglais (or Walk of the English) was officially adopted by the city authorities.

Site Archéologique Gallo-Romain (Archaeological Site of Gallo-Roman Nice)

The Roman city of Nice, Cemenelum, was the capital of the Alpes-Maritime province and is said to have had a population of about 20,000.

The Musée Archéologique, sitting amongst the excavated Roman remains in the Cimiez district, displays finds from this site and others from the Alpes-Maritimes *département*, ranging from prehistory to the early Christian era. Numerous domestic artefacts, including beautifully decorated pottery, indicate the sophistication of their lifestyle, but the highlight has to be the intricate 1st-century AD bronze Masque de Silène. The extant Roman buildings around the museum (in the lee of the Matisse Museum) are part of the large baths complex.

Nearby, but separate from the Site Archéologique, is Arènes (the arena), a diminutive, elliptical amphitheatre with a 4,000-spectator capacity. Gladiators once faced each other in mortal combat here, but today the arena plays host to festivals and concerts.

160 avenue des Arènes, 06000 Nice. Tel: 04 93 81 59 57. Open: Wed–Mon, 10am–6pm. Closed: some public holidays. Bus nos 10, 15, 17, 22, 25. Admission fee.

The promenade des Anglais flanks Nice's pebble beach

Walk: Central Nice

This circular walk links a range of Nice's central attractions, from the old quarter to the latest museums. You will also experience the many architectural styles found in the city.

Allow 2 hours.

Start at the city tourist office, at the start of the promenade des Anglais. Walk west, away from the city centre, to view the elegant façades of the landward side of the promenade, until you reach the Negresco hotel.

1 Hotel Negresco
An abiding image of Nice since it opened its doors in the early 1900s, this is still one of the classiest places in town.
Cross the street and walk east back along the beach side of the promenade.

2 Promenade des Anglais
You can now take in the landward buildings from a distance and also watch the activities on Nice's beach, a pebble rather than sand strand. The wide promenade is always a hive of activity. Joggers have their own 'super highway' while elegant *niçoises* ladies coo over babies, or sigh at the couples enjoying a romantic tryst.
Cross back across the promenade des Anglais where it becomes quai des États-Unis. Walk away from the seafront, on the right-hand side of avenue des Phocéens for 50 or so metres (before it turns into boulevard Jean Jaurès) until you reach rue St François-de-Paule. Turn right here and walk down to the marché aux Fleurs and Cours Saleya.

3 Nice Market
This is just about the liveliest place in the city and a feast for your senses, with mouth-watering aromas and a riot of colour. Do not forget to take in a little history too! You will pass Église St-François de Paule on the left and the *belle-époque* Opéra Municipal (1885) on the right. Also on the left, before the market, the Baroque Chapelle de la Miséricorde is on Cours Saleya.
At the far end of Cours Saleya, turn right then left into rue des Ponchettes. At the top you will find, on the left, the way to the top of Colline du Château.

The *avant-garde* Modern Art Museum

4 Colline du Château

The castle hill has excellent views of the old town and Baie des Anges, with small areas of ancient ruins to explore.
Walk down the shady hill by taking montée Lesage, then allée Professeur Benoît, which leads into allée François Aragon. At the junction of montée du Château and allée François Aragon take the flight of steps (Escalier Ménica Rondelly) back down into the old town at place Ste Claire. Take a right along rue de la Providence which runs into rue Neuve to place J Toja. From here walk down avenue St Sébastien to the museum.

The terracotta rooftops of old Nice give way to elegant 19th-century façades

5 Modern Nice

Here you will find some of the best modern architecture, the *avant-garde* square library and the Musée d'Art Moderne et d'Art Contemporain, with its collection of late 20th-century art.
From the museum, walk left down avenue Félix Faure back towards the coast.

6 Gardens and Fountains

The avenue is flanked by fine 19th-century buildings, while to the left the land has been transformed into a series of green squares with gardens and fountains, the best being place Masséna. Walking through this area leads directly back to the promenade des Anglais, to complete your walk.

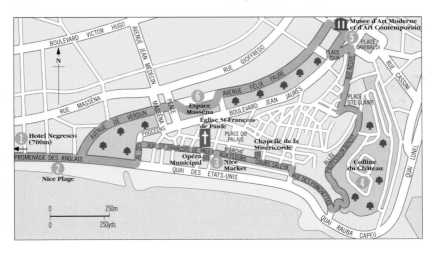

Monaco and Monte-Carlo

Set on a narrow coastal strip backed by a steep escarpment, Monaco's name is inextricably linked with money, success and fun – its sporting events and gambling are famed throughout Europe. Independent fiefdom of the Grimaldi family since 1215, the principality is a throwback to the feudal era. It works closely in many ways with France, but is independent from it.

A well-groomed guard watches over the Palais Princier

Several districts make up the whole – the rock of Monaco is the original citadel, La Condamine the port area, Monte-Carlo the 19th-century extension and Fontvielle the late 20th-century suburb.

THE ROCHER DE MONACO (Rock of Monaco)

The historic heart of the principality sits atop an impressive rock plateau 80m (260ft) high. An elegant district of 18th-century houses, their façades painted salmon pink and cream, it is a conservative district, home to the oldest Monégasque families. Native Monégasques number fewer than 10,000.

Cathédrale de Monaco

You may be surprised at the lack of references to Princess Grace as you stroll around the principality. The restrained reverence of the people is typical of the Monégasque character. You will be able to stand over the simple tomb of the princess in Monaco Cathedral.

This elegant white stone church was built in 1875 to replace a 13th-century chapel. Aside from the tomb, which rests

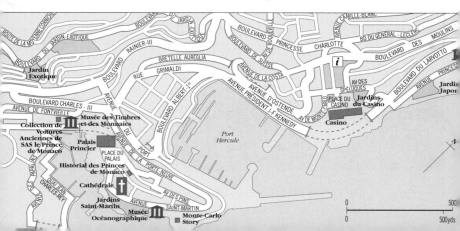

alongside those of other Grimaldi princes and princesses in the neo-Romanesque apse, note the main altarpiece of St Nicolas by Louis Bréa (1500).
Rue Colonel Bellando de Castro 4, 98000 Monaco. Tel: 377 93 30 87 70. Bus nos 1, 2. Free.

Historial des Princes de Monaco/Musée des Cires (Story of the Princes of Monaco/Wax Museum)

The family history of the princes of Monaco is traced through a series of dioramas featuring wax figures dressed in authentic historic costumes.
Rue Basse 27, 98000 Monaco. Tel: 377 93 30 39 05. Open: Mar–Sept, 10am–6pm; Oct–Feb, 11am–5pm. Bus nos 1, 2. Admission fee.

The Monte-Carlo Story

This multivision film relates the development of the principality from the small rock of Monaco to one of the pleasure capitals of Europe.

Terrasses du parking du Chemin des Pecheurs, 98000 Monaco. Open: Jan–June, 2–5pm; July–Aug, 2–6pm; Sept–Oct, 2–5pm. Closed: 1 Nov–25 Dec. Bus nos 1, 2. Admission fee.

Le Musée Océanographique et Aquarium (Museum of Oceanography and Aquarium)

The most impressive building in Monaco, seemingly rising directly out of the 85m (280ft)-high rock face, this museum was inaugurated in 1901 by Prince Albert I as an institute for ocean research. Albert was an avid scientist who undertook his own oceanographic expeditions, and his specimens form the basis for a rather charming, if quaint, natural history collection set in a marvellous Art Deco hall. Modern methods of oceanographic research are also examined.

The aquarium is one of the finest in Europe, displaying over 200 species with around 4,000 fish in environments from tropical to temperate. Highlights include

Tiny Monaco rests on a rocky plateau

A crowd gathers in the place du Palais for the daily changing of the guard

summer. Behind the staircase, the *galerie à l'italienne* (Italian style gallery) replete with 17th-century frescoes, links several state apartments. The highlight of the tour is the ceremonial Salon du Trône with its Renaissance chimneypiece.

In one wing of the palace is a museum safeguarding the archives of the principality, including the Charter of Independence signed by King Louis XIII of France, and an extensive collection of 'Napoléonia'.

Outside, in the place du Palais, you can watch the ceremonial relève de la Garde des Carabiniers (Changing of the Guard) at 11.55 each morning. *Place du Palais, 98000 Monaco. Tel: 377 93 25 18 31, www.palais.mc. Open: June–Sept, 9.30am–6pm; Oct, 10am–5pm. Closed: Nov–May. Bus nos 1, 2. Admission fee.*

the re-creation of a coral reef, a shark lagoon and a micro-aquarium (plankton and microscopic fauna that are the ocean's first link in the food chain). *Avenue Saint-Martin, 98000 Monaco. Tel: 377 92 16 77 93. Open: Jan–Mar, 10am–8pm; Apr–June, 9.30am–7pm; July–Aug, 9.30am–7.30pm; Sept, 9.30am–7pm; Oct–Dec, 10am–6pm. Bus nos 1, 2. Admission fee.*

Palais Princier (Prince's Palace)
Home of the Grimaldi family and seat of power since 1215, the palace has been extended several times but particularly during the Renaissance. At the heart of the complex is the Cour d'Honneur, an immense square famed for its 17th-century marble staircase, where orchestral concerts are held during the

JACQUES COUSTEAU (1910–97)

In the 1940s, Jacques-Yves Cousteau was fascinated by the underwater world but frustrated by the limited time he could stay there. Cousteau invented the 'aqualung', now universally known as SCUBA (Self Contained Underwater Breathing Apparatus). This allowed divers to take their own air under the water with them, so they could stay down longer and dive deeper.

Cousteau went on to introduce the aquatic environment to a generation of television viewers, and to pioneer underwater camera work, when he filmed his subsequent submarine expeditions.

MONTE-CARLO

Monte-Carlo put the fizz into Monaco. This 'new town' was designed and laid out in the 19th century when the rock became overcrowded. With the success of the casino, it quickly developed a reputation for glitz and glamour. The downtown district is characterised by a series of elegant avenues and manicured squares, whilst areas of recently redeveloped Monte-Carlo have sports facilities and luxury hotel developments.

Monte-Carlo Casino

Designed by Charles Garnier, architect of the Paris Opéra, and built in 1878 (with later additions), the casino is in many ways the *raison d'être* of Monte-Carlo.

The richly decorated interior is the epitome of opulence with a wealth of gold leaf, ornate plasterwork, bas-reliefs, frescoes and sculptures. The marble atrium, with its 28 onyx columns, sets the scene for the individual gaming rooms.

Casino Square, where the high-rollers alight from their chauffeur-driven vehicles, is the social hub of Monte-Carlo. On one side of the square is the Hôtel de Paris built in 1864, a legend in its own right with a string of historical and contemporary celebrity guests. *Monte-Carlo Casino, place du Casino, 98007 Monaco. Tel: 377 92 16 20 00. Open: from 12pm (noon). Over-21s only in the gaming rooms (take ID or passport). Correct attire required (no shorts, sandals or T-shirts). Bus nos 1, 2, 6. Admission fee.*

Jardin Japonais (Japanese Garden)

Over 7 hectares (17 acres) in size, this park of lakes, ponds and cascades

Monaco's fortifications date from the 14th century

The port of La Condamine separates Monaco and Monte-Carlo

interspersed by manicured Japanese maples and pagodas is carefully designed to meet strict Shinto principles of balance. It is one of the largest authentic Japanese gardens outside the Land of the Rising Sun and a haven of tranquillity in a busy city.
Avenue Princess Grace, 98030 Monte-Carlo. No phone. Open: 9am–sunset. Bus nos 4, 6. Free.

Musée National d'Automates et Poupées d'Autrefois (National Museum of Dolls and Automata)

Another splendid Garnier-designed mansion now houses this unique collection of automata (moving mechanical devices made in imitation of a human being) made in Paris at the end of the 19th century.

Avenue Princess Grace 17, 98030 Monte-Carlo. Tel: 377 93 30 91 26. Open: Easter–30 Sept, 10am–6.30pm; Oct–Easter, 10am–12.15pm, 2.30–6.30pm. Closed: 1 Jan, 1 May, 19 Nov, Christmas Day. Bus nos 4, 6. Admission fee.

FONTVIELLE

The youngest district of Monaco, Fontvielle was reclaimed from the sea during the 1980s. It is predominantly a residential quarter, and careful urban planning has allowed for the inclusion of several community projects, including the Stade Louis II, home to Monaco football club but also used by schools and amateur sports associations. The district also has a couple of interesting attractions.

Exposition de la Collection de Voitures Anciennes de S.A.S. le Prince de Monaco (Royal Vintage Car Collection)

The Grimaldi family have always had a penchant for hot cars and their extensive collection of over 100 veteran, vintage and later cars includes a 1903 De Dion Bouton, the first motor vehicle owned by the family, a 1929 Bugatti and a 1986 Lamborghini Countach.

Terrasses de Fontvielle, 98000 Monaco. Tel: 377 92 05 28 56. Open: 10am–6pm. Closed: 25 Dec. Bus nos 5, 6. Admission fee.

Musée des Timbres et des Monnaies (Museum of Stamps and Money)

Monaco's independence is brought into focus with this collection of stamps and money issued by the principality.

Flamboyant decoration is the trademark of the Monte-Carlo Casino

principality, the Jardin Exotique exhibits over 6,000 species of arid and semi-arid plants with spectacular gigantic cacti and grasses, plus exceptional views along the coast.

The grotto, 60m (200ft) below ground, comprises several limestone caverns with mature stalactites and stalagmites. Evidence of prehistoric habitation came to light during excavations and the finds are now on display in the museum amongst other prehistoric remains, including human burials dating from the Palaeolithic to the Bronze Age.

Jardin Exotique de l'Observatoire et Musée d'Anthropologie Préhistoire, boulevard du Jardin Exotique, 98000 Monaco. Tel: 377 83 15 29 80, www.monte-carlo.mc/jardinexotique. Open: 15 May–15 Sept, 9am–7pm; 16 Sept–14 May, 9am–dusk. Closed: 19 Nov and 25 Dec. Bus no 2. Admission fee.

Stamps have been produced since 1885, while the numismatic collection displays coins, notes and medallions issued since 1640.

Terrasses de Fontvielle, 98000 Monaco. Tel: 377 93 15 41 50. Open: 1 July– 30 Sept, 10am–6pm; 1 Oct–30 June, 10am–5pm. Bus nos 5, 6. Admission fee.

Other attractions
Jardin Exotique, Grotte de l'Observatoire et Musée d'Anthropologie Préhistoire (Exotic Garden, Observatory Grotto and Prehistoric Anthropology Museum)
Inaugurated in 1933 and planted against steep rock faces on the heights above the

TAX EXILES IN MONTE-CARLO

Residents of Monaco pay far less tax than other Europeans and for this reason the principality has become popular with the super-rich from entrepreneurs to sports stars. Tennis player Boris Becker lived here for a while, and it is home to most of the Formula 1 Grand Prix drivers.

However, it is not just the tax saving that lures celebrities. It is also the fact the Monégasques are not in the least star-struck and do not hound their well-known faces for autographs, allowing them to live a relatively normal life.

Walk: Monaco to Monte-Carlo

This linear walk leads you from the seaward side of the rock of Monaco round the harbour to the heart of Monte-Carlo, taking in the ever-changing urban landscape of the principality.

Allow 4 hours.
Start at the Aquarium.

1 Musée Océanographique

This magnificent living and historical marine collection was the legacy of Prince Albert I, who had a passion for oceanography. Do not forget to take in the coastal views from the terrace.
Leave the Aquarium and travel left down avenue Saint-Martin, where you will find the white-and-gold façade of the cathedral on your right.

2 Cathédrale

Final resting place of Princess Grace, the neo-Romanesque cathedral has some

Monaco's narrow streets

fine paintings from the Nice School, best of which is the altarpiece by Louis Bréa, which were transferred from the 13th-century church that the cathedral superseded.
Turn right, and right again, from outside the cathedral and walk along rue de l'Église until it meets rue Émile-de-Loth. A left along here brings you out into the place du Palais.

3 Place du Palais

The huge square is normally quiet, but in the lead-up to the changing of the guard (*daily at 11.55am*) a large crowd gathers. Arrive at least 30 minutes before this time if you want a front-row view. The tour of the Palais des Princes takes visitors through the ceremonial and state rooms of what is also the Grimaldi home.
From the palace take a left to the place du Palais parapet for views over the port at La Condamine. To your left (between the palace and the parapet) is an arch. Pass under this and follow the walkway, Rampe Major, to walk down from the rock to the port.

4 Rampe Major

This was the main entry to Monaco and

the palace for many centuries. You will pass under an early Renaissance gateway just after leaving the square.

After setting off down Rampe Major, you will leave the main path at the public toilets. Walk past the toilets through the parkland and across avenue de la Porte-Neuve to bring you out at the intersection of avenue du Port and boulevard Albert I which runs alongside the harbour.

The 21st-century principality with its high-rise living

5 Port

Some of the most expensive ocean-going properties along the Riviera moor here. There is always a bustling nautical atmosphere along the quayside, but this is also a favourite area for events such as boat shows and car launches.

Walk along the quayside, then take avenue d'Ostende, which climbs up the far side of the port. This leads into the Monte-Carlo district. Keep right, where the road splits, taking avenue de Monte-Carlo. This will bring you out directly into place du Casino.

6 Casino

The southern façade of the Casino, directly ahead, is your first glimpse of its incredible ornate detail. Once in the square, you will probably be dodging Ferraris and Lamborghinis to catch a glimpse of the main façade (do not forget that this is a public roadway, so watch out for traffic). You can go inside provided you are dressed appropriately. After your visit, have a drink at one of the cafés in the square or head to the bar at the Hôtel de Paris for some celebrity-spotting!

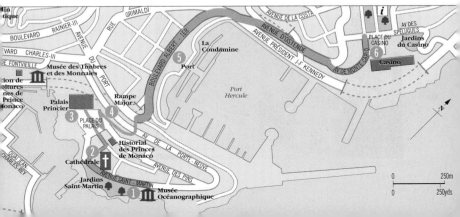

Few people knew the exact location of Monaco, or its lineage, in the late 1950s. But when the conventional and rather homely Prince Rainier won the heart of Grace Kelly, considered one of the world's most beautiful women and an Oscar-winning actress at the height of her career, it caused an intense interest in the principality that has yet to fade away.

This tiny rock, whose income is mainly from offshore banking and gambling, has a much longer pedigree than Hollywood's. In 1297, François Grimaldi was expelled from Genoa during internecine strife. In fact, he escaped the city dressed as a monk, an act commemorated on the principality's coat of arms, and arrived in Monaco. In 1308 he bought the land from the Genoese, and he and his family expanded along the coast, becoming feudal lords of several communities.

This does not mean that they have had things all their own way. Monaco was always too small to survive as a totally independent entity, especially as it stood betwixt the powerful duchies of southern France and northern Italy at a time when borders were in constant flux. It was occupied several times, most importantly by the Spanish between 1524 and 1641, when they made its ruler a prince and the small rock became a principality – the status it holds today. Also, although the princes of Monaco have always been Grimaldis, the bloodline is not a direct descent. It has come through several different European houses and is currently with the House of Polignac.

And life has not always been a bed of roses for Grimaldi rulers. Prince Jean II was murdered by his brother Lucien in the 1500s, and in 1604 Honoré I was thrown

1956. The 'Hollywood' connection made this conservative town cool, even after Grace's tragic death in 1982.

In the celebrity-obsessed late 20th and early 21st centuries, their three children live every day under the intense scrutiny of the European paparazzi. Their antics always make the front pages, whether it is heir Albert's apparent reluctance to marry and produce the next generation of little princes, Stephanie's eclectic taste in men or Caroline's mystery scalp condition, yet as Prince Rainier reaches his twilight years the family continues to carry out its official duties with great decorum and they remain hugely popular with their people. Though their role as overlords is anachronistic, some may say obsolete, their subjects do not seem the least bit interested in changing the status quo.

into the sea by his disgruntled subjects, the kind of direct action that would be unimaginable for the conservative Monégasques today.

Despite the glamorous veneer, being ruler of a principality is a serious business. The family's responsibilities are strangely like those of a Chief Executive Officer of an industrial conglomerate and they take them very seriously. But still, it is hard to imagine how the late 20th century would have panned out for Monaco had the prince not met the 'showgirl' at the Cannes Film Festival and their romance not resulted in marriage in

Opposite and above: Likenesses of Princess Grace in oils and bronze
Below: The princess carried on her love affair with acting by becoming patron of her own Monaco theatre

The Corniches – Nice to the Italian Border

This short section of coast – between Nice and the Italian border, including the principality of Monaco (*see pp108–13*) – was the original French Riviera, as described by travellers during the late Victorian age. The fine villas they built and the genteel resorts they founded still welcome upmarket vacationers.

The great and good are celebrated with fine statues

Corniches

East of Nice, cliffs rise steeply almost directly from the coast.

Three parallel 'corniche' (ledge) roads run towards the Italian border. The upper road or *grande corniche*, built by Napoléon on the route of the old Roman road, links several medieval hilltop villages and offers exceptional views down to the coast below (captured in the 1955 Alfred Hitchcock film *To Catch a Thief*, starring Cary Grant and Grace Kelly).

The lowest of the three, the *corniche inférieure*, completed as late as the 1880s, hugs the coastline, linking the resorts.

Beaulieu-sur-Mer

This tiny fishing village was discovered by American tycoon Gordon Bennett in the late 19th century and transformed into an elegant resort, with some exceptional turn-of-the-century villas and hotels.

Villa Grecque Kérylos is the most unusual. Its typically Aegean exterior hides a surprising interior, the accurate re-creation of a 2nd-century BC Greek villa. The beautifully crafted rooms – complete with mosaics, frescoes and typical furniture – were created using ancient techniques and the finest raw materials. It was built by the archaeologist Théodore Reinach, who used genuine amphorae and statues for the finishing touches.

Villa Grecque Kérylos, 06310 Beaulieu-sur-Mer. Tel: 04 93 01 44, www.villa-kerylos.com. Open: 3 Feb–30 June, 10am–6pm; July–Aug, 10am–7pm; 1 Sept–2 Nov, 10am–6pm; 3 Nov–2 Feb, Mon–Fri 2–6pm, weekends and French school hols 10am–6pm. Admission fee.

Cap Ferrat

Nicknamed 'the millionaire's peninsula', Cap Ferrat real-estate was snapped up by the cream of European society in the 19th century. Villa Ephrussi-di-Rothschild is the *pièce de resistance*, a magnificent *belle-époque* Italianate mansion designed for Baroness Ephrussi-di-Rothschild. Inside, her discerning eye can be seen in the substantial collection of art and furniture, from Gobelin tapestries and Sèvres porcelain to Fragonard canvases.

Her Impressionists Gallery contains pieces by Monet, Renoir and Sisley. The extensive grounds have some of the finest formal gardens to be seen in southern France.

Villa Ephrussi-di-Rothschild, 06230 St-Jean-Cap-Ferrat. Tel: 04 93 01 33 09, www.villa-ephrussi.com. Open: 3 Feb– 2 Nov, 10am–6pm; 3 Nov–2 Feb, Mon–Fri 2–6pm, weekends and French school hols 10am–6pm. Admission fee.

Eze

One of the most renowned medieval citadels along the Riviera, Eze lives up to the hype. Set on a rocky pinnacle with majestic views over the coast, the village is a maze of narrow, cobbled lanes and fortress-like stone houses, surrounded by an imposing curtain of walls. You enter through *la poterne*, a 14th-century postern gate. Within the village, craft shops now proliferate in what used to be wine cellars and stables. The oldest building is the Chapelle de Saint Croix

(also known as Chapelle des Pénitents Blancs) dating from 1306. The medieval mansions of Eze's wealthier residents are now top-class hotels, including the Château Eza, former residence of Prince William of Sweden.

Seemingly suspended over the terracotta rooftops at the top of the village is the Jardin Exotique (Exotic Garden), set in the grounds of the ruined château with some exceptional cacti, agaves and aloes.

Le Jardin Exotique, place du Général de Gaulle, 06360 Eze. Tel: 04 93 41 10 30. Open: 1 July–31 Aug, 9am–8pm; 1 Sept– 30 June, 9am–6pm. Admission fee.

Menton

The most easterly town along the Riviera, Menton rubs shoulders with its Italian neighbour Ventimiglia to the east. The area has an exceptionally mild microclimate, with more cloud-free days than anywhere along the coast. The town is famed for its principal

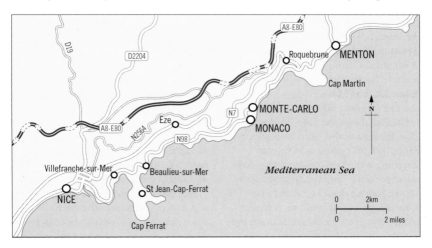

The waterfront at Villefranche-sur-Mer

Menton's Musée des Beaux-Arts du Palais Carnolès (Fine Arts Museum), in what was once a Grimaldi summer mansion, boasts a da Vinci. It is surrounded by a fragrant orchard (Jardin d'Agrumes) specialising in citrus fruit, the most important such collection in Europe. In the orchard, contemporary sculptures are displayed.

Menton is renowned for its Lemon Festival, held annually on Shrove Tuesday.

Salle de Mariages, place Ardoïno, 06506 Menton.
Tel: 04 92 10 50 00.
Open: 10am–12pm, 2–6pm.
Closed: Tue and official holidays.
Admission fee.
Musée Jean Cocteau, Vieux Port, 06506 Menton. Tel: 04 93 57 72 30. Open: 10am–12pm, 2–6pm. Closed: Tue and official hols. Admission fee.
Musée des Beaux-Arts, avenue de la Madone 3, 06506 Menton.
Tel: 04 93 35 49 71. Open: 10am–12pm, 2–6pm. Closed: Tue and official holidays. Free.

cash crop, lemons, and its range of exuberant and exotic gardens.

The 53-m (174-ft) Genoese tower of Basilique St Michel (St Michael's Basilica) dominates an old town of tall pastel buildings. Consecrated in 1675, its façade and interior have exceptional Baroque decoration.

Menton is firmly linked with the artist, writer and film director Jean Cocteau (1889–1963), who spent the final years of his life here. He was invited to design the Salle de Mariages (Wedding Room) at the Town Hall, a room that now displays vast surreal frescoes on the walls plus lighting and furniture to the artist's blueprint. The Musée Jean Cocteau is housed in a 17th-century stone bastion on the waterfront. Here an eclectic collection of works shows his versatility.

Roquebrune (Cap-Martin)

You will find what is reputed to be the oldest olive tree in the world at the entrance to Roquebrune, but this is not the only superlative you can use to describe the place. This Carolingian fortified village is the most complete of its kind in Europe.

Designed to confuse an enemy as much as possible, should they infiltrate the outer defences, Roquebrune is a three-dimensional labyrinth of stone

Afternoon sunlight reflecting on the walls at Menton

houses and narrow arcaded alleyways, as rue Moncollet shows.

The *donjon* (keep) at the top of the village was the feudal stronghold and is now a small museum. From here there are sweeping views down to Cap Martin with its 19th-century estates.
Donjon, 06190 Roquebrune-Cap-Martin. Tel: 04 93 35 07 22.
Open: Feb–June, 10am–12.30pm, 2–6pm; July–Aug, 10am– 12.30pm, 3–7.30pm; Sept–Oct, 10am– 12.30pm, 2–6pm; Nov–Jan, 10am–12.30pm. Admission fee.

The *corniche inférieure* hugs the coastline

Villefranche-sur-Mer
Set on one of the prettiest natural harbours along the Riviera, Villefranche was founded in 1295 on the site of a Roman port. A monumental citadel (1557) sits on the seaward side, protecting the pretty quayside and its distinctive pastel façades. The citadel houses five museums, ranging from artefacts from a 16th-century Genoese ship that sank in the harbour to a series of modern sculptures by Antoniucci Volti.

The small old town lies by the quayside. Its highlight is rue Obscure, a 13th-century covered alleyway, 130m (420ft) long and reminiscent of an oriental souk, which once ran alongside the medieval ramparts.

The short quayside welcomes both fishermen and cruise-ship passengers and is lined with cafés. The fishermen traditionally worshipped at the 14th-century Chapelle de Saint Pierre, site of a remarkable renovation project overseen by Cocteau in 1957. His frescoes, scenes from the life of St Peter, now cover the interior walls.
Citadel, Fossé de la Citadelle, 06230 Villefranche-sur-Mer. Tel: 04 93 76 33 27. Open: June, 9am–12pm, 3–6pm; July–Aug, 10am–12pm, 3–7pm; Sept, 9am–12pm, 3–6pm; Oct–May, 10am–12pm, 2–5pm. Closed: Tue, Sun mornings and all Nov. Free. Chapelle de Saint Pierre, Quai Amiral Courbet, 06230 Villefranche-sur-Mer. No phone. Open: June–Sept, 10am–12pm, 3–7pm; Oct–May, 10am–12pm, 3–5pm. Closed: Mon. Admission fee.

Walk: Central Menton

This circular walk links all the major attractions of Menton, whilst also allowing you to enjoy the views along the seafront and the heart of the town.

Allow 3 hours.

Start from the waterfront. There is a large car park just next to the Musée Cocteau.

One of the artists's mosaics at the entrance to the Cocteau Museum

1 Musée Cocteau

Set in a defensive bastion on the harbour. Here you can enjoy the artist's wide ranging output, from paintings and drawings to ceramics and tapestries. *Leave the museum, turn left and walk across the parkland of the Esplanade de Francis Palmëro to the Promenade du Soleil. Continue along the seafront, enjoying the views across the bay to Cap Martin. Leave the coastline at Elizabeth Square, 2km (1¼ miles) from the start, then cross avenue du Général de Gaulle to the Musée Beaux-Arts.*

2 Musée Beaux-Arts

The museum houses a small collection ranging from the 13th to the 20th century. Highlights are the *Virgin and Child* by da Vinci and a *Virgin and Child with St Francis* by Bréa. Spend time exploring the Jardin d'Agrumes (citrus garden) and the sculptures on display, ranging from classical to avant-garde. *Leave the garden and walk back towards the town on the avenue de la Madone. Keep walking as the name changes to avenue Carnot, then avenue Félix Faure. When you reach the junction with avenue de Verdun, you will see the Jardin Biovès on the left. This is the prime location for activities during the Lemon Festival. The tourist office is also here. Continue on your way as the road turns into rue St-Michel, the pedestrian-only street that*

The Baroque bell tower of the Basilique St-Michel dominates old Menton

The Jardin d'Agrumes has a fine collection of citrus fruit

links the new town with the old town. Turn left at rue de la Mairie and you will see the town hall just to the left at the next intersection.

3 Mairie

The town hall is where you will find Cocteau's Salle de Mariages, with its dramatic and faintly bizarre frescoes; the furniture and light fixtures were also designed by the artist.

Leave the town hall and walk left down rue de la République, which becomes rue Général Galliéni. As the road sweeps left around the Chapelle des Pénitents Noirs, look for an alley on the right next to rue de Bréa. Take this alley and a first right

on a stepped walkway called rue de la Conception. This leads to the Chapelle des Pénitents Blancs and Basilique St-Michel.

4 Basilique St-Michel

This is one of the finest Baroque churches on the Riviera, with a distinctive pastel façade and ornate interior. Several generations of the Puppo and Vento families, local artists, have decorated most of the altarpieces in the 12 small chapels.

From the square in front of the basilica take a left, then left again down the steps of the rue des Écoles Pie, keeping right through the square and down another flight of steps to rue des Logettes. A right here leads to rue St-Michel at place du Cap.

5 Rue St-Michel

This is the main artery linking old and new Menton. A pedestrian-only thoroughfare for most of its length, lined with shops and cafés, it is an atmospheric place to stroll, especially in the evenings.

From place du Cap it is a short walk down rue des Fours to the bastion and back to the Cocteau Museum.

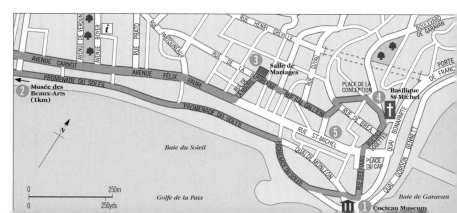

Inland from Nice

Leave the crowded coastal *corniche* and within 30 minutes you enter an agricultural region with terraced fields and scattered villages leading up to the mountains of the pre-Alps. Religious art abounds in the churches of these mountain settlements and the countryside is a green lung for city-dwellers, who flock to enjoy the fresh air and outdoor pursuits.

Window boxes are an apartment dweller's garden

La Brigue

Owned by the Lascaris family throughout the Middle Ages, La Brigue was at the heart of many local conflicts. The family's ruined château survives but the main attraction in the town is the collegiate church of St-Martin. Dating from the 16th century, it has an outstanding collection of paintings from the Nice Primitive School, including three canvases by Louis Bréa.

Coaraze

The medieval village of Coaraze, with its many covered alleyways, crowds atop a rock outcrop at the centre of a wooded valley. The narrow alleyways and small squares are decorated with sundials designed by Cocteau, Ponce de Léon and Valentin amongst others. The Chapelle Notre-Dame-de-la-Pitié, also known as Chapelle Bleue, is decorated with frescoes by Ponce de Léon (1962), depicting scenes from the life of Christ.

Gorges du Paillon

The River Paillon has carved a short and very accessible gorge below the villages of Peille and Peillon. The site, with its narrow walls, natural tunnels and sink-holes, is popular with 'canyoners' – gorge-walkers and climbers.

Gorges de la Vésubie

The River Vésubie makes a dramatic last statement before it is swallowed by the mighty River Var on its journey to the Mediterranean. It has cut a gorge with sheer walls up to 60m (200ft) high. In places only 25m (80ft) wide, it weaves its way northeastwards into the Mercantour National Park. The D2565 road runs through the depths of the gorge, offering dramatic views of the multi-coloured rock strata, best viewed on a sunny day.

Gorbio

A gigantic elm tree planted in 1713 marks the entrance to Gorbio. The medieval village with its cobbled lanes and 16th- and 17th-century houses is perched on a majestic site high above Roquebrune and Cap Martin, surrounded by olive groves and verdant gardens.

Lucéram

Nestled in a gorge at the top of the Peillon Gorge and surrounded by the vast Peïra-Cava forest, Lucéram was for centuries a fiefdom of the count of Nice. The parish church of St Marguerite is its highlight, with France's most complete collection *in situ* by the Nice School. The main altarpiece, the *retable Sainte Marguerite* painted by Louis Bréa *c.* 1500, now has an ornate Baroque frame. The altarpieces of St Pierre and St Paul, attributed to Canevasio, were painted in the late 1400s. The church has a rich treasury, the finest piece being the silver statue of Ste Marguerite, the town's patron, fighting the dragon (*c.* 1500).

There are excellent views over the town from the church terrace. Vaulted, cobbled alleyways lead up from the valley. Amongst the secret corners and

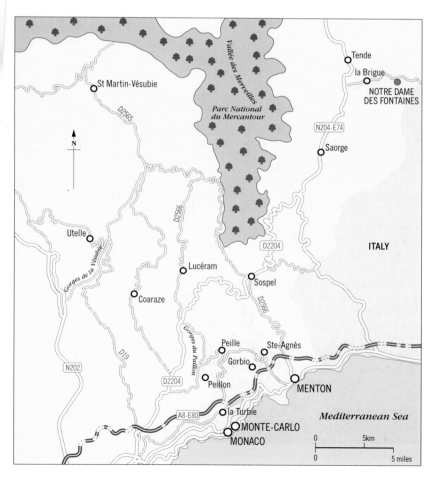

The Gorges du Paillon are a popular place for canyoning

grottoes are over 100 *crèches* (nativity scenes). The once fine castle has been reduced to some crenellated curtain wall and one lonely 16th-century tower.

In the surrounding hills two small chapels, Chapelle St-Grat and Chapelle Notre-Dame-de-Bon-Coeur, are richly decorated with late 15th-century frescoes attributed to Jean Balaison. *Église Sainte-Marguerite. Open: 9am–12pm, 2.30–6pm. Free.*

Notre Dame des Fontaines

Constructed in the 15th century in the remote hills above La Brigue, this tiny chapel built in Piedmontese style is

Retable in the church of Sainte-Marguerite in Lucéram

famed for its ornate interior, blanketed by rich frescoes. Those in the chancel are by Canevasio, a renowned early Renaissance artist, and depict biblical scenes, though the figures are wearing late medieval costume.
For opening times, contact the Office du Tourisme at place Saint Martin, 06430 la Brigue. Tel: 04 93 04 36 07.

Peille

Clinging to the side of a valley wall, Peille is an old village but still thriving in the 21st century. Set against a backdrop of three jagged peaks, the village consists of several small squares linked by narrow, tiled alleyways, leading to a vantage point at the top of the village. The 13th-century Chapelle St-Sébastien, with its unusual rounded Romanesque roof, now houses the Mairie (Town Hall), whilst the 13th-century parish church displays a 16th-century altarpiece with panels by Honoré Bertone.

From Peille, you can leave the car and take the Via Ferratta, a strenuous combination of hiking and climbing with sections of rope bridges, into the surrounding hills (*return trip approx 3 hours*).

Peillon

Set on a towering rocky outcrop, Peillon truly lives up to its nickname of the *nid d'aigle* (eagle's nest). There are dramatic views up to the village as you approach, with the houses seemingly extensions of the sheer rock face, huddled together as if to stop each other from falling to the valley below.

The peak was occupied in the Iron Age but 'modern' Peillon was established in the 10th century, when coastal dwellers moved inland to escape the Barbarian invasion. The houses or *écailles* they built were the first medieval dwellings in the region.

The 15th-century Chapelle des Pénitents Blancs has rich frescoes by the Piedmontese painter Canevasio (*c.* 1495), depicting eight scenes from the Passion with the figures dressed in medieval costume.

A pretty cobbled square with a fountain designed in 1789 by the then Geometer Royal, Ghiotti, signals the end of the road. The pedestrian-only Carrera Centrala leads you to the top of the village, 376m (1,233ft) above sea level, with views down the valley.

Saorge

This sturdy mountain town cascades down a hillside of the Roya valley and is approached from the south along the Gorges de Saorge, where the road sweeps under overhanging rocks alongside the River Roya.

Narrow winding roads lead into the Riviera hinterland

Considered impregnable in the Middle Ages, the narrow alleyways of the old town contain Madonna de Poggio, a Romanesque chapel that is the oldest place of worship in the region (sadly not open to the public).

Monastère de Saorge (Saorge Monastery), founded by the Friars Minor of the Observance (Franciscans) in 1633, enjoys a fine setting amongst verdant woodland close to the town. The tour includes the Baroque church and the cloisters, with 18th-century frescoes of scenes from the life of St Francis.

Monastère de Saorge, 06540 Saorge. Tel: 04 93 04 55 55. Open: 1 Apr–31 Oct, 10am–12pm, 2–6pm; 2 Nov–31 Mar, 10am–12pm, 2–5pm. Closed: Tue, 1 Jan, 1 May, 1 Nov, 11 Nov and Christmas Day. Admission fee.

Sospel

Historic crossroads for alpine and Italian routes, Sospel was one of the region's most prosperous communes in the Middle Ages. The town declined in importance in the 17th and 18th centuries, leaving a wealth of historic buildings, including 15th-century *lavoirs* (wash houses).

Spanning the Bévéra River, the 13th-century Pont-Vieux with its stone towers is the emblem of the town. The 16th- and 17th-century arcades on either bank were built to protect from floods two old districts, where you will find a wealth of 17th-century architecture; but rue de la République (once the main street, rue Longue) still has some 14th- and 15th-century buildings. Saint Michel, one of the largest religious buildings in Alpes-

---

THE SALT ROAD THROUGH SOSPEL

Throughout the Middle Ages, the now-Italian region of Piedmont (then a duchy) bought salt from mines in Provence, a lucrative trade of over 5,000 imperial tonnes a year at its peak. Delivery involved mule caravans across the mountain passes. The *autoroute* of its day, through the Col de Tende via Sospel, became known as the Salt Road. Towns along the way benefited from the passing trade, acting as the 'service areas' of their time.

Maritimes, has an exceptional vaulted ceiling. Started in 1641, it has several important Primitive altarpieces. Place Saint-Michel, on which the church is set, has some outstanding Baroque façades.

Just 1km (less than 1 mile) outside the town, Fort St Roch was built in the 1930s as an extension of the Maginot line. Situated 50m (160ft) below ground, the fort was designed to be self-sufficient for weeks on end. You can tour the underground corridors and kitchens, and study the small museum relating the story of the Alpine Corps during the Second World War.

Fort St Roch, 06380 Sospel. Tel: 04 93 0414 41. Open: Apr–June, Sat–Sun and holidays 2–6pm; July–Sept, Tue–Sun 2–6pm; Oct–Nov, Sat–Sun and holidays 2–6pm. Closed: Nov–end Mar. Admission fee.

St Martin-Vésubie

The leading town of the central Mercantour and a centre of outdoor pursuits, St Martin-Vésubie sits nearly 1,000m (3,280ft) up, in the heart of verdant forest.

It is easy to see why Peillon is nicknamed 'eagle's nest'

Very popular with hikers, climbers and those seeking the 'great outdoors', the town has an attractive old quarter seen at its best in rue du Docteur-Cagnoli, the main artery, flanked by medieval houses. The Baroque parish church, Madone de Fenestre, has panels from an altarpiece by Bréa. The 12th-century statue of Madone de Fenestre spends winter here, and summer at a chapel higher in the mountains.

Ste-Agnès

The highest-perched coastal village in Europe, 760m (2,500ft) above the sea, Ste-Agnès surveys the coast of the *corniche* from its rocky roost. The panorama is a main attraction, but the village is a picturesque tangle of cobbled alleyways of which rue Longue is typical.

Protected for many years by its location, Ste-Agnès was picked for that reason in the 1930s, when a fort was built here as part of the Maginot line to defend the main routes from Italy and easterly sea approaches to Toulon and Marseille. This modern citadel is an interesting contrast with the medieval fortresses scattered across the area.

THE MAGINOT LINE

During the 1930s as talk of war grew more and more vociferous, the French decided that the best form of deterrent would be to build a 'Great Wall of China' defence to keep the Germans out. They embarked on a vast building programme of concrete fortresses from the Belgian border to the Italian border.

At the outbreak of war the series of fortresses, named the Maginot Line after the then minister of war André Maginot, was not complete and the Germans simply invaded France through the gaps.

Tende

Set at 816m (2,677ft), this high mountain settlement nestles in a valley below the Riba de Bernou on an ancient route. The grey-slated houses cascade down the hillside on either side of the arterial road, an important link with Italy since the first millennium.

The 15th-century Eglise Collégiale Notre Dame de l'Assomption, with its richly decorated façade and frescoes, is the architectural highlight, and Tende is also home to the Musée des Merveilles. Even if you cannot make time to tour the Vallée des Merveilles (*see p132*) itself, you should visit this museum with its modern façade. It has reproductions of many of the carvings, as well as domestic artefacts found at the site and information on the lifestyle of these ancient peoples.

Tende is now a centre for outdoor sports, being an eastern gateway into the Parc du Mercantour (*see pp134–5*).

Musée des Merveilles, avenue du 16 Septembre 1947, 06430 Tende. Tel: 04 93 04 32 50, www.museedesmerveilles.com Open: 2 May–15 Oct, 10am–6.30pm; 16 Oct–30 Apr, 10am–5pm. Closed: Tue, 12–24 Mar, 13–25 Nov, 1 Jan, 1 May and Christmas Day. Admission fee.

La Turbie

Founded on the *grande corniche* at the base of the Tête de Chien overlooking Monaco, la Turbie is the site of the

'It's first on the left, or is it the right?'

most majestic and impressive Roman structure along the Riviera. The Trophée des Alpes (Alpine Trophy) was erected in the 1st century BC to commemorate the victories of Emperor Augustus over the peoples of the Alps. The colonnade of fine Doric columns, set on a high plinth, supported a huge statue of the emperor, which could be seen all along the coast.

After the fall of the Roman Empire the trophy was looted, then used as a coastal defence, before being partially reconstructed with the financial support of American Edward Tuck. The on-site museum has a model of the trophy as it looked in its heyday and has information about the renovation programme.

Eglise St-Michel-Archange in the town was built in the 18th century and has a fine Baroque interior featuring paintings by Veronese and Van Loo.
Trophée des Alpes, avenue Albert I 18, 06320 La Turbie. Tel: 04 93 41 20 84. Open: 1 Apr–20 June, daily 9.30am–6pm; 21 June–20 Sept, daily 9.30am–7pm; 21 Sept–31 Mar, Tue–Sun 10am–5pm. Closed: 1 Jan, 1 May, 1 Nov, 11 Nov, Christmas Day. Admission fee.

Utelle

Set high above the Vésubie valley and relatively isolated even today, Utelle is still imbued with medieval character, with its narrow alleyways and ruined château, though its churches are the main interest. The Gothic porch of 14th-century Eglise St-Véran has carvings of the legend of St Veranus,

while the simple lines of the interior are enhanced by later decoration, including the main altar with scenes from the Passion and the *retable de l'Annonciation* (altarpiece of the Annunciation) by a member of the Nice School. The nearby Chapelle des Pénitents Blancs has a *Descent from the Cross* by Rubens.

Even higher above the village is the Chapelle de la Madone d'Utelle, a place of pilgrimage since its founding in 850 by Spanish sailors – though the church is 19th-century. The nearby view is one of the most impressive in the Riviera.

Vallée des Merveilles (Valley of Marvels)

One of the largest and most important sites of prehistoric art in Europe, covering over 10 hectares (25 acres), the Vallée des Merveilles features over 37,000 images of tools, weapons and geometric figures carved onto the rocks.

They were the work of the Ligurian peoples, who inhabited this remote place (actually three valleys) below Mount Bego in the early Bronze Age.

Some carvings are accessible by footpath (*allow about 3$\frac{1}{2}$ hours for the round trip*) but the best examples are in a protected area where the public must be accompanied by a qualified guide. *Qualified guides can be booked through the Office du Tourisme de la Haute-Roya – Tel: 04 93 04 73 71 (allow 8 hours) – or contact Destination Merveilles – Tel: 04 93 73 09 07, www.destination-merveilles.com – who organise daily walking tours.*

The Trophée des Alpes was once a potent symbol of Roman power

Drive: Into the Parc National du Mercantour

This circular tour contrasts the capital of the Riviera with the vast unspoilt panoramas of the southern Mercantour and its mountain communities, returning to Nice via a couple of medieval hilltop villages.

Allow 8 hours.

Leave Nice by travelling west along the coast on the N98 then inland via the N202. This is the main route into the hinterland, leading to the winter and summer resorts of the Mercantour, pre-Alps and Alps. Turn right at the junction of the D2565 and you will immediately enter the Gorges de la Vésubie.

1 Gorges de la Vésubie

The road sits in the very depths of the gorge alongside the River Vésubie with its many twists and turns. The gorge narrows to only a few metres wide in places and the sheer walls rise over 60m (200ft) high. *At the head of the gorge, turn left on the D32 to Utelle.*

2 Utelle

Utelle was remote in its hilly location between the Vésubie and Tinée valleys

There are 20 towns and villages in the Mercantour National Park

until recent times. Visit Eglise St-Véran for its porch and main altar, and nearby Chapelle des Pénitents Blancs for its *Descent from the Cross* by Rubens, before continuing on to the Chapelle de la Madone d'Utelle for the exceptional views.

Return to the D2565 and continue into the Vésubie valley (left) through Lantosque, before turning right across the river on the D70 in the direction of the Col de Turini.

3 Fine Landscapes

This road climbs quickly into the lower Mercantour and to some of the finest landscapes of the journey. The col itself at 1,604m (5,273ft) is a little disappointing: its winter mountain lodges and ski runs look a little dour in the middle of summer.

At the Col de Turini, turn right on the D2566 in the direction of Lucéram.

4 Approach to Lucéram

Sections of this drive have been damaged by recent forest fires but they do not spoil the views as you approach the town itself, which nestles in a cleft in the valley.

Stop here to study the exceptional panelled altarpieces painted by Bréa and Canevasio, and also to explore the village and its *crèches* (nativity scenes). *Continue south on the D2566 to l'Escarène and leave the village on the D21, direction Peillon.*

5 Gorges du Paillon

Not as dramatic as the Vésubie, this is the place for some easy walking with sets of metal ladders linking the various different levels. Unfortunately, a large aggregate factory spoils the lower valley. *Turn left at the D53 where the road climbs to Peille.*

6 Peille

Surrounded by jagged peaks, this medieval community continues to thrive. The 13th-century parish church displays a 16th-century altarpiece.
Leave the village the way you came, returning to the D21. Take a left and then left again after 2km (1¼ miles), when the road climbs to Peillon.

7 Peillon

The approach to this tiny village offers several picturesque views before the road runs out and you must enter the village on foot. Canevasio's frescoes at the 15th-century Chapelle des Pénitents Blancs (*c.* 1495) depict scenes from the Passion. There are views down the valley from the top of the village.
Return to the D21, then take a left at the junction with the D2204, which leads back into Nice to complete the trip.

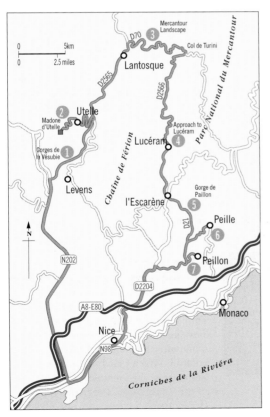

Excursions

MARSEILLE

The largest port in the Mediterranean and France's second city, Marseille is huge and sprawling. Founded by the Greeks in the 6th century BC, it was a thriving Roman port and its importance has been built on Mediterranean trade ever since.

The closest port to France's African colonies, the city has accepted numerous immigrants, particularly after Algerian independence in the 1960s, and its multi-ethnic population adds tremendous diversity to the city but also simmering racial tensions – this is where right-wing activist Jean-Marie le Pen cut his political teeth.

Despite (or because of) its rather unsavoury reputation for corruption and drug trafficking, Marseille has a unique atmosphere, a gritty urban feel that does not exist anywhere else on the

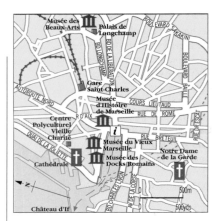

Marseille has one of the largest fishing fleets in France

Riviera. There are significant attractions too, mostly gathered close to the port and the old town.

Basilica Notre Dame de la Garde

The golden statue of Madonna and Child atop the basilica has been protecting Marseille from the highest point in the city since the 1830s, on the site of a 13th-century place of pilgrimage.

The basilica takes its name from 'the Guard' – the 154-m (505-ft) hill that is a natural early-warning station for the city, being an excellent viewpoint for its land and sea approaches. Eventually the church became part of a formidable citadel, dismantled only in the second half of the 20th century.

Built of fine pale Cassis stone, the basilica is smaller than one would imagine: the interior seems crowded with pews and a forest of marble columns. The highlights are the remarkably vivid mosaics of the life of the Virgin Mary. The one in the cupola above the apse shows the boat in which, it is said, Mary was washed ashore at Marseille.

There are excellent views over the city from the surrounding terrace.
13281 Marseille. Tel: 04 91 13 40 80. Open: winter, 7am–6.30pm; summer, 7am–7.30pm. Bus no 60. Free.

Cathédrale de la Nouvelle Major

This neo-Romanesque church is the largest built in France in the 19th century and, despite the publicity given to Notre Dame de la Garde, it is Marseille's major place of worship and resting-place of the bishops of Marseille.

The interior is a really successful re-creation of a Byzantine place of worship. Rather dark and sombre on first impressions, it is crammed with rich detail of inlaid semi-precious stones and rare marbles.
Place de la Major, 13002 Marseille. Open: daily 8am–6pm. Closed: Sun am for services. Bus nos 49a, 83. Free.

The Musée des Beaux-Arts

Château d'If

Set on a tiny island 2km (1¼ miles) southwest of the port, the formidable Chateau d'If was built as a protective bastion in the 16th century but was later converted into a notorious prison. Conditions were described in detail in Alexander Dumas' famous story *The Count of Monte Cristo*, when the eponymous hero was locked up here.
Ferry trips from the old port. GACM Quai des Belges, 13000 Marseille. Tel: 04 91 55 50 09, www.ansaweb.net/gacm. Admission fee. Boat tour departs 9am, 12 noon, 2pm and 3.30pm, although during the summer there are later departures. Check with tourist information.

Musée des Beaux-Arts (Fine Art Museum)

The Musée des Beaux-Arts building was designed as a municipal *palais* rather than a private palace. It dates from 1870 and was built on the site of the Château d'Eau, where water, diverted from the River Durance and used for the city's drinking water, entered the municipality. The palais was designed by Espérandieu.

Housed in the left wing of the palace, the museum has two main strengths: the French, Italian and Flemish gallery with paintings by Rubens, Courbet and Pérugin; and the 17th to 20th-century Provençal school with works by Puget, Serre and Mignard.
Palais Longchamps, 13004 Marseille. Tel: 04 91 14 59 30. Open: 1 June– 30 Sept, 11am–6pm; 1 Oct–31 May, 10am–5pm. Metro: Longchamp–Cinq-Avenues. Admission fee.

Musée des Docks Romains

A rare find for archaeologists, this Roman warehouse was discovered with its consignment of *dolia* (earthenware jars for storage of oil or wine) still inside. In addition to the fascinating building and its merchandise, the museum displays other items relating to trade in the city between the 6th century BC and the 4th century AD.
Place Vivaux, 13002 Marseille.
Tel: 04 91 91 24 62. Open: 1 June–30 Sept, 11am–6pm; 1 Oct–31 May, 10am–5pm.
Metro: Vieux Port. Admission fee.

Musée d'Histoire de Marseille

The spectacular re-creation of a 3rd-century BC shipwreck welcomes you to this interesting collection, charting the development of the city up to the 19th century. It includes the results of excavations during recent redevelopment of the city centre.
Centre Bourse, 13001 Marseille.
Tel: 04 91 90 42 22. Open: 1 June–30 Sept, 11am–6pm; 1 Oct–31 May, 10am–5pm. Metro: Vieux Port.
Admission fee.

Musée du Vieux Marseille

A small collection of artefacts concentrates on the oldest district of the city, with drawings and paintings depicting daily life around the busy

The daily fish market on the quai des Belges

port and on the narrow old streets.
*Maison Diamantée, rue de la Prison,
13002 Marseille. Tel: 04 91 55 28 68.
Open: 1 June–30 Sept, 11am–6pm;
1 Oct–31 May, 10am–5pm. Metro:
Vieux Port. Admission fee.*

Centre de la Vieille Charité
Built in the 17th century as a workhouse
for the poor and designed by Pierre
Puget in the style of a medieval
monastery, the centre is now home
to two of the finest museums in the
south of France.

**Musée d'Arts Africains, Océaniens,
Amérindiens** is a collection

Mending nets is a regular chore

amalgamating several donations of
high-quality ceremonial artefacts,
including African sculptures, decorated
Mundurucu skulls from the South
American rainforest and Haïda native-
American masks from British Columbia.

Musée d'Archéologie Méditerranéenne
offers an exceptionally rich selection of
artefacts shedding light on a series of
civilisations, from the local Celto-Ligurian
civilisation of the 3rd century BC to
the classical Greek. The museum is
particularly strong on Egyptian artefacts,
from the Old Empire to the Coptic
Christians of the 1st millennium.
*Centre de la Vieille Charité, rue de la
Charité 2, 13002 Marseille.
Tel: 04 91 14 58 80. Open: 1 June–30
Sept, 11am–6pm; 1 Oct–31 May, 10am–
5pm. Metro: Juliette. Admission fee.*

WHY IS THE FRENCH NATIONAL ANTHEM CALLED LA MARSEILLAISE?

When the people of Marseille heard that
revolution was brewing in Paris, 600
volunteers set out from the city to lend their
support. As they travelled, they sang the
Hymn of the Army of the Rhine, composed
by Rouget de l'Isle, to keep their spirits up.
Parisians also found the song uplifting and
it became a rallying song for the city.

After the fall of the monarchy, a new
national anthem was needed and popular
opinion decided the hymn should be it, but
it was re-christened *La Marseillaise* in honour
of the Marseille contingent.

Walk: Old Marseille

Known to everyone as Le Panier (the breadbasket), old Marseille – to the east of the port – is a district of narrow lanes and alleyways lined with tall 16th- to 18th-century houses. Generations of immigrants have found their first home on French soil here and it is still a vibrant, multi-ethnic, residential quarter filled with small corner shops, cafés and tiny squares, where local residents gather and children play.

Allow 3 hours.

Start your tour at the quai des Belges (2 min walk from the Office du Tourisme).

1 Port

Rather too large to be picturesque, the old harbour was the beating heart of the city for centuries but now caters only to small pleasure boats and the fishing fleet. The quai des Belges at the head of

La Vieille Charité – designed to imitate medieval cloisters

the port is the location of the renowned morning fish market – one of the best in France.

Leave the quayside at the Hôtel de Ville (Town Hall) and make your way to place Jules Verne behind the building, where you will find the Musée du Vieux Marseille.

2 Musée du Vieux Marseille

Housed in one of the oldest mansions in Marseille (1570), the museum has various depictions of Le Panier through the ages and holds temporary exhibitions of Provençal crafts.

From the museum, continue along the rue du Lacydon, take a left and you are immediately into place Vivaux, where you will find the Musée des Docks Romains.

3 Musée des Docks Romains

Marseille was an important port during the Roman era and this impressive warehouse, complete with the amphorae carried by ships to all corners of the empire, really helps bring this trade to life.

*On emerging, turn left down rue de la
Loge. At the junction with rue H Tasso,
take a right to reach place de Lenche,
from where the narrow rue de la
Cathédrale leads to Cathédrale la Major.*

4 Cathédrale la Major

This impressive neo-Romanesque
cathedral is indeed the city's major
centre of worship. Its dark interior,
chandeliers and mosaics bring to life
the sort of Christian basilica found
all across the empire of Byzantium.

Look for the 12th-century chevet of
the Vieille Major, to the left of the main
entrance of the cathedral. This is all that
remains of the previous cathedral.
*Turn left out of the main entrance of the
cathedral, then left on avenue Robert
Schuman. Turning right on to the short
rue A Becker leads to place des 13
Cantons. From here follow rue du Petit
Puits, which meets rue de la Charité,
home of the La Vieille Charité complex.*

Notre Dame de la Garde watches over the old city

5 La Vieille Charité

The complex hosts two museums, with
high-quality artefacts beautifully
displayed. The Musée d'Arts Africains,
Océaniens, Amérindiens concentrates on
ceremonial artefacts from native peoples
from Africa, Pacific basin and the
Americas. Musée d'Archéologie
Méditerranéenne has collections from
Mediterranean and near eastern ancient
civilisations, including the Greek
diaspora and Egypt.
*Take a left on leaving, and follow rue de la
Charité to place Lorette. Turn right into rue
Fontaine Neuve, then almost immediately
left into rue St-Antoine, across the small
gardens and into place Sadi-Carnot. This
is on rue de la République, the grand
boulevard that bounds the old town.
Walking (right) down rue de la République
leads back to the port and the ornamental
gardens inland of quai des Belges.*

Bouillabaisse

This supreme southern French dish began as a humble fisherman's meal made with whatever was left over when the fish market closed. It fell out of favour with restaurateurs, but survived the onslaught of *haute cuisine*, coming back into fashion in the 1990s. Descriptions of bouillabaisse as 'fish soup' do not do it justice. It is a full meal – not for the small stomached.

The name bouillabaisse comes from the Provençal *bouï abaisso* meaning 'boil and press'. Each fishing port along the coast had its own recipe, incorporating slightly different ingredients. The most authentic is regarded as that of Marseille, if only because the city still has a thriving fishing community, something that has been lost on other parts of the Riviera with the depletion of fishing stocks.

Recipe

To make bouillabaisse you will need a mixture of fish (a minimum of four different types) totalling 4kg (9lb) for 6 people from the following: *rascasse* (scorpion fish), *rascasse blanche*, *araignée vive* (live spider crab), *rouget grondin* (red mullet), *Saint-Pierre* (John Dory), *lotte* (monk fish), *fielas* (conger eel), *chapon* (scorpion fish), *cigale de mer* or *favouille* (small green crabs) or *langouste* (crayfish), plus 1kg (2¼lb) of fish sold under the name *petits poissons de roche* or small rock fish. It is important that the fish are fresh: do not forget that authentic bouillabaisse was made with fish caught that morning!

Other ingredients you will need are good-quality, extra-virgin olive oil, good-quality saffron, garlic, onions, fennel, parsley, tomatoes and potatoes.

Cooking

You willl need a base stock for your bouillabaisse. For this, cut the *petits poissons de roche* into chunks and add the crabs, chopped tomatoes, onions and garlic, and 2 tablespoons of olive

oil. Heat for 10–15 minutes, then add 4 litres (7 pints) of water and let simmer for 30 minutes.

Pour the base through a sieve and *moule* (a type of sieve which grinds the fish and bone) to ensure a smooth consistency, then add the remaining olive oil, the firm-fleshed fish (whole) and enough water to cover the fish. Boil for 12 minutes. Add the soft-fleshed fish (whole) and cook for another 6 minutes.

To serve

There are two ways to serve bouillabaisse. You can remove the large fish, slice them and then serve them on a separate plate, or leave the bouillabaisse complete. In either case, the broth should be poured into bowls over bread coated with *aioli* (garlic mayonnaise) or *rouille* (blend of hot red peppers, garlic and mayonnaise-style paste of pounded bread).

Despite bouillabaisse being a 'poor' or working-man's dish, using readily available ingredients, it has a high reputation; but standards have suffered as fish stocks have declined. Restaurants substitute cheaper and less authentic ingredients (such as vegetable oil and cheap saffron), so some restaurants in Marseille have got together to create the 'Bouillabaisse Charter', pledging to remain true to the original recipe. Eat bouillabaisse in the following restaurants and you will know you are getting the genuine article.

Le Caribou, place Thiers 38, 13001 Marseille. Tel: 04 91 33 22 63, www.lecaribou-corse.com
Chez Caruso, Quai du Port 150-162, 13002 Marseille. Tel: 04 91 90 94 04.
Chez Fonfon, Vallon des Auffes 140, 13007 Marseille. Tel: 04 91 52 14 38, www.pageszoom.com/fonfon
L'Epuisette, Anse de Vallon des Auffes, 13007 Marseille. Tel: 04 91 52 17 82, www.l-epuisette.com
Le Miramar, Quai du Port, 13002 Marseille. Tel: 04 91 91 10 40, www.bouillabaisse.com
Le Rhul, corniche J F Kennedy 269, 13007 Marseille. Tel: 03 91 52 01 77.

Oppposite: Fresh fish at a local restaurant
Above: Bouillabaisse makes a hearty meal

Getting Away From It All

The Riviera is one of the busiest and most densely populated parts of France, swelled by hundreds of thousands of visitors, especially in the summer months. However, it is surprisingly easy to escape the crowds. Whether you choose to get out into the great open spaces, take a boat trip or a scenic rail journey, you can find your own quiet spot.

Directions to the great outdoors

Parc National du Mercantour

Year-round playground for the inhabitants of the Riviera, this national park was created in 1979 and covers a vast 70,000 hectares (270sq miles) of the Nice hinterland, stretching north into the pre-Alps with their mountain peaks.

Over 2,000 species of plants thrive here, 220 of them rare examples and 40 endemic here. This is the only place in Europe where the moufflon, chamois and ibex live together, along with golden eagles, deer, stoats, foxes, wild horses, blind moles and a rare cave salamander.

The park is divided into two sections: the core zone, where nature comes first, and the areas around this where man and nature live together. This region has over 20 towns and villages that now act as bases for visiting walkers, hikers and mountaineers. Cross-country skiing stations in the south, and two alpine skiing stations, add interest in the winter.

The park also contains the Vallée des Merveilles (*see p132*), and the associated Musée des Merveilles – explaining the finds – is found in Tende (*see p131*) on the eastern boundary.

Park headquarters, rue d'Italie, BP 1316, 06006 Nice. Tel: 04 93 16 78 88, www.parc-mercantour.fr. Information offices at the following towns: St Martin-Vésubie and Sospel.

RETURN OF THE WOLF AND VULTURE TO THE MERCANTOUR

Much of European wildlife has been wiped out by hunting – a sport still enjoyed by the French – but there have been attempts to redress the balance in the Mercantour. The reintroduction of bearded vultures began in 1993, and a small but stable population is now well established (look out for the huge creatures 'thermalling' in the summer skies).

Wolves needed no such help from man. It is thought that they made their way to the national park from Italy in the late 1980s, but they have chosen to stay because of the excellent environment and ample food supply.

Îles d'Hyères

Lying just off the coast opposite the town of Hyères, these three islands are also known as the Îles d'Or ('islands of gold'), due to their shiny shale rocks.

Settled by the Greeks during the 5th century BC, they became Church property in the 5th century AD, before developing into a pirate enclave during the Middle Ages. Later, under the French Crown, they acted as a strategic defence for Toulon harbour to the west. Today, barely populated, they offer excellent walking.

Île de Porquerolles, the largest of the group, is 7km by 3km (4 by 2 miles). The private domaine of Belgian entrepreneur Joseph Fournier for much of the 20th century, it was planted with a vineyard and exotic orchards. Most of the island, though, is protected by the Conservatoire Botanique National Méditerranéen, to preserve the woodland and plants that thrive here. Fort Ste-Agathe (1810) has a small museum on the history of the islands.

Much of neighbouring Île de Port-Cros has also been designated a National Park. It is hilly and boasts some unusual walks, including an underwater path marked with information about the marine flora and fauna, for those with masks and snorkels.

Much of Île du Levant, the smallest island, is military property and off limits

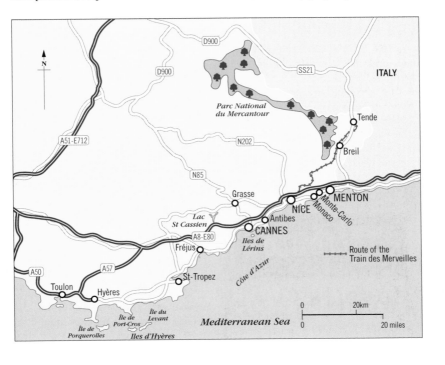

to the public. Heliopolis at the western tip is a favourite place for naturists.

Take drinking water with you to all the islands. There is no smoking outside the villages.

Ferries from Hyères with Transports Littoral Varois (TLV). Tel: 04 94 57 44 07; from Le Lavandou with Vedettes des Îles d'Or. Tel: 04 94 71 01 02; from the Giens peninsula with TLV (as above).

Îles des Lérins

Lying in the Golfe Juan just offshore from Cannes, the two islands make a splendid excursion, though you will not usually have them to yourselves.

Île Sainte-Marguerite, the larger island, sits only a kilometre or so off the mainland. Fort Royal, built by Richelieu and fortified by Vauban, is where the Man in the Iron Mask was incarcerated from 1687 to 1698. The identity of the unfortunate fellow has never been ascertained, but theories range from an ancestor of Napoléon to an illegitimate brother of Louis XIV.

One museum in the fort is dedicated to the Huguenots, explaining the history and the fate of these 17th-century Protestants in Catholic France. Another

Ferries from Cannes make the short trip to the Îles des Lérins

is a Musée Maritime, displaying finds from Roman and Saracen shipwrecks.

Île Saint-Honorat is the private property of the Monastère St Honorat, founded during the 4th century by St Honoratus and now occupied by a brotherhood of Cistercians. The fortified keep of the Ancien Monastère was built at the time of Saracen attacks and is set on a rocky outcrop on the southern shore, with a later chapel and cloister. The Monastère Moderne is 19th-century, with 11th- and 12th-century elements. Visitors can tour the museum and the church.

Year-round ferries to Île Sainte-Marguerite from Cannes harbour with Compagnie Esterel Chanteclair. Tel: 04 93 39 11 82. Ferries to Île Saint-Honorat from Cannes harbour with Société Planaria. Tel: 04 92 98 71 38.

Lac de St Cassien

This man-made reservoir holding irrigation water lies between Fréjus and Grasse, and draws many people for freshwater sports – anglers, rowers, kayakers and canoeists. Areas of the lakeside are set aside for swimming and beach activities.

Bis routes avoid congested areas

Le Train des Merveilles

Inaugurated in 2002 on the Nice–Breil–Tende line, the Train des Merveilles links several medieval hill towns in the Breil-sur-Roya valley and the lower Mercantour area, including Peille, Sospel and Saorge. You can book guided tours of your destination (on certain days of the week) or feel free to wander at your own pace. There is entertainment on board the train as you journey.

Tickets from the train station in Nice, no need to make a reservation.
Tel: 08 92 35 35 35, www.sncf.com. A daily service, May–Sept, departs Nice at 9.24am. Oct–Apr, Sat and Sun only.

Val de la Siagne

One of the last hidden corners of the Riviera, the route between Saint-Cézaire and Mons – a single-track road – offers exceptional views of the Siagne Valley and its gorge, plus a landscape of ancient, terraced olive groves once common in the south of France and now almost wiped out.

Mons is a tiny 10th-century enclave ravaged by plague and then repopulated in the 1460s. The medieval village has been well preserved as a vital community, with rather fewer of the galleries and souvenir shops found in similar settlements closer to the coast. The parish church dates from the 12th century, with 17th-century additions, and has a rather oversized but impressive Baroque altarpiece (1680). Place St-Sébastian (once the site of the château) has an exceptional view over low hills carpeted with oak forest, with the coastline from Menton to Toulon clearly visible on a fine day.

The Val de la Siagne is only a stone's throw from the crowded coast

Shopping

Do not leave home without a generous allowance for souvenirs, as the Riviera has some of the finest products in the world. You can spend hours browsing along the cobbled alleyways of inland villages or the wide boulevards of its towns and cities. It is enough to cause credit-card meltdown!

Earth and wood: a shop inspired by nature

What to look for

Where Picasso and Matisse once rested their easels, you will find dozens of today's artists and there is even more choice in commercial galleries. Many concentrate on Provençal landscape and life, others on the avant-garde. Centres of excellence include St Paul, Vence, Eze and Tourrettes-sur-Loup.

Handicrafts too are an art form here, with even the most mundane item produced with an eye for beauty. This is where in the 1970s Terence Conran found his inspiration for the Habitat homeware shops.

Pottery is the most obvious, with objects from oil pourers to egg cups (Vallauris is a centre for pots), but equally you will find hand-blown glassware (particularly at Biot) and olive-wood bowls and coasters. Other items for the house include table linen made from vivid blue and yellow Provençal fabrics (once fashioned into skirts or *jupes de Provence*, almost a uniform for country women though now falling out of favour).

Perfume production continues, with several companies in Grasse manufacturing their own fragrances, but soap production has an equally long tradition with *savon de Marseille* being a by-word for quality throughout France. Olive-oil soap, perfumed soaps and body products can be found all across the region.

Not only is it important to smell good, but looking good is *de rigueur* too. The French invented haute couture and the Riviera has some of the most expensively clad bodies in the world – even when attired in a skimpy bikini. You will find all the best (and best-known) designer names here, especially at Cannes, Nice, Monaco and St Tropez, as well as hundreds of smaller boutiques and myriad T-shirt emporia.

Ask for your tax back!

For non-EU residents who intend to make expensive purchases, it is possible to recover the Value Added Tax (currently 19.6%) on most items. Any bill for goods totalling over 182.94 euros is eligible. You must fill out a form at the store (you will need your passport) and hand this form to the customs officer for approval (they may want to see the goods). Refunds follow in a few days direct to your bank or credit card account.

SHOPS
Art
Art-Thé
Gallery featuring the work of several local artists, plus café for drinks and snacks. *Place Mariejol 3, 06600 Antibes. Tel: 04 93 34 44 41.*

Atelier à Deux
Commercial gallery of local artists concentrating on Provençal landscapes. *Rue Grande 30, 06570 St Paul de Vence. Tel: 04 93 32 97 55.*

La Galerie Jouvène
Featuring the work of landscape artist G Goloubetski. *Avenue Victor Hugo 25, 13260 Cassis. Tel: 04 42 01 96 33.*

La Vie en Douce
Traditional hand-painted religious icons and Provençal *santons. Grand'rue 5, 06140 Tourrettes-sur-Loup. Tel: 04 93 59 29 17.*

SANTONS

Traditional Provençal souvenirs are *santons*, painted clay figurines representing the characters of the nativity scene, now found nowhere else in France. They originally became popular in the region during the Revolution when religious worship was suppressed. The name *santon* is derived from *santoun*, the Provençal for 'little saint'. Once the *santons* were out of sight in people's homes but today they are displayed with great pride (particularly in the Mercantour villages such as Lucéram) and hand-painted examples can prove quite expensive.

Clothing
Body Art
Boutique with designer names such as Paul Smith and Jean-Paul Gaultier. *Rue Sibilli 30, 83990 St Tropez. Tel: 04 94 97 16 05.*

Cargo
Boutique stocking the latest unisex fashions. *Rue Gambetta 1, 06236 Villefranche-sur-Mer. Tel: 04 93 76 76 90.*

Hélène Chenard
Hand-woven scarves, shawls, jackets and ponchos using natural fibres. *Grand'rue 10-12, 06140 Tourrettes-sur-Loup. Tel: 04 93 59 36 36.*

Dior
Collections of haute couture from one of the oldest French houses. Also in Nice and St Tropez. *Boulevard de la Croisette 38, 06400 Cannes. Tel: 04 92 98 98 00.*

Ferragamo
Exceptional shoes started the Ferragamo empire, but now it is clothing and accessories too. Also in Monte-Carlo.

Colourful crafts make ideal souvenirs

Rue Notre Dame 9, 06400 Cannes.
Tel: 04 93 38 29 75.

Hermès
Designer clothing and accessories by this upmarket name. *Avenue de Verdun 8, 06000 Nice. Tel: 04 93 87 75 03.*

K Jacques
Hand-made Tropezian leather sandals and other hand-made shoes. *Rue Allard 25 (also at rue Mermoz 3 and rue Seillon 16), 83990 St Tropez. Tel: 04 94 54 83 63.*

La Rose des Vents
Hand-made hats to add panache to any outfit. *Rue Grand 35, 06570 St Paul de Vence. Tel: 04 93 32 80 52.*

Crafts
Catherine et André Adelheim
Hand-made porcelain and other pottery. *Rue Costillon, 83440 Mons. Tel: 04 94 85 36 75.*

L'Air du Sud
A full range of the locally made pottery. *Avenue Georges Clémenceau 47, 06220 Vallauris. Tel: 04 93 64 03 22.*

L'Artisan du Cristal
Cut-glass and crystal objects, including traditional chandeliers. *Place Général du Gaulle, 06360 Eze. Tel: 04 93 64 90 65.*

Bazarettes
Objects made of Cassis stone. *Rue du Jeune Anarchasis 4, 13260 Cassis. Tel: 04 42 01 34 25.*

Boutique des Maures
Range of locally produced pottery and handicrafts. *Place du Marché, 83310 Port Grimaud. Tel: 04 94 56 26 50.*

Boutique le Moulin
Olive wood items, soaps and pot-pourris made in the region. *55 rue Carnot, 83230 Bormes-les-Mimosas. Tel: 06 74 18 27 04.*

Cant d'Or Ceramiques d'Art
Unusual hand-thrown and decorated pottery with 'Fabergé-like' ceramic decoration. Bowls, animals and jewellery. *18 rue Carnot, 83230 Bormes-les-Mimosas. Tel: 04 94 71 84 08.*

Centre de Rencontre des Arts Occitans
Artists' collective featuring potters, *santon*-makers, enamellers and decorative artists. *Galerie de la Muscadière, Voie-Aurélienne-La Tour de Mare, 83600 Fréjus. Tel: 04 94 44 42 55.*

Création Mosaique
Creations in mosaic, including tables and smaller decorative items. Mosaic workshops available. *Rue Désaugiers 3, 83600 Fréjus. Tel: 04 94 51 09 88.*

Fabrique de Pipes Courrieu
Traditional pipes made from wood of the Massif des Maures. *Avenue Georges Clémenceau, 83310 Cogolin. Tel: 04 94 54 63 82.*

Maison Gault
Miniature hand-painted Provençal houses that you can collect and arrange into villages. *Place de la Fontaine 41, 06570 St Paul de Vence. Tel: 04 93 32 50 54.*

Gabriel Mariani
Sculptor in bronze and wood. *Le vieux Logis, Carriea Centrala 2, 06440 Peillon. Tel: 04 93 79 91 37.*

Poterie Augier
Traditional mansion now filled with traditional pottery. *Rue Clémenceau 19, 83990 St Tropez. Tel: 04 94 97 12 55.*

Aux Saveurs de Provence
Cork and pottery objects, plus excellent chestnut food products. *Boulevard Caminat 1, 83610 Collobrières. Tel: 04 94 28 17 32.*

Verrerie de Biot
Hand-blown glassware – watch the artisans at work. *Chemin des Combes, 06410 Biot. Tel: 04 93 65 03 00. www.verreriebiot.com*

Perfumes
Fragrances de Provence
Fifty different fragrances plus soaps and body products. *Rue Grand 39, 06570 St Paul de Vence. Tel: 04 93 32 65 67.*

Kalliste
Produces *Eau de Menton* amongst other fragrances. *Rue de la Marne 1, 06506 Menton. Tel: 04 93 41 45 87.*

Parfumerie Fragonard
Signature fragrances by the famed perfume house (also at Eze). *Boulevard Fragonard 20, 06130 Grasse. Tel: 04 93 36 44 65.*

Other local goods
La Boutique de Léa
Provençal fabrics by the metre, or made-to-measure items such as tablecloths. *Espace Sainte-Claire, 06570 St Paul de Vence. Tel: 04 93 32 68 05.*

Cartier
One of the most famed names in jewellery and watches (also in Monaco). *Avenue de Verdun 4, 06000 Nice. Tel: 04 92 14 48 20.*

La Compagnie de Provence
Traditionally produced soaps made with 72 per cent olive oil, and other body products. *Rue de Caisserie 1, 13000 Marseille. Tel: 04 91 56 20 94.*

Galerie Artagra
Varied antiques and small *objets d'art* as well as paintings. *Rue des Templiers 14, 83310 Grimaud. Tel: 04 94 56 80 11.*

Soleil de Provence
Very good selection of Provençal material, tablecloths, napkins etc. *Rue Saint Antoine 21, Le Suquet, 06400 Cannes. Tel: 04 93 38 28 75.*

Louis Vuitton
Designer luggage and accessories as used by the famous. *Boulevard de la Croisette 22, 06400 Cannes. Tel: 08 10 81 00 10.*

Marc Zinardelli
Exceptional hand-made leather handbags and purses. *Rue St Sebastian 42, 06410 Biot. Tel: 04 93 65 16 46.*

Entertainment

The Riviera has an excellent range of entertainment throughout the year, with the winter programme concentrated in the larger towns and cities but a summer schedule that takes in the full range of communities, both on the coast and inland. The programme is so full that it is only possible to scratch the surface with the following information. For comprehensive details contact the appropriate tourist office.

Live jazz at Juan-les-Pins

NIGHTLIFE
Clubs
You can find discos and clubs at all the coastal resorts, though the best are at Monte-Carlo, Cannes and St Tropez, where you may find yourself sharing your dance floor with actors, pop stars or supermodels. Here are the do not miss locations.

L'Ambassade
Rue de Congrès 18, 06000 Nice.
Tel: 04 93 88 88 87.

Cat Corner
Rue Macé 22, 06400 Cannes.
Tel: 04 93 39 31 31.

Jimmy'z
Sporting Club of Monte-Carlo, avenue Princess Grace 26, 98001 Monte-Carlo.
Tel: 377 92 16 22 77.

Les Caves du Roy
Avenue Maréchal Foch, 83990 St Tropez.
Tel: 04 95 56 68 00.

Cinema
French cinema has a long tradition, it varies from the comedies of Jacques Tati to the dramas of François Truffaut, and it is still thriving with a reputation for highbrow and art-house productions, explorations of the psyche or sexual peccadilloes.

France gets all the latest 'lower-brow' Hollywood blockbusters but the government takes stringent measures to ensure the continued health and purity of the French language. Instead of subtitles, the French insist on dubbing all dialogue into French so, though you may be watching Keanu Reeves or John Travolta, at most cinemas you will be listening to a French actor saying their lines.

The following cinemas show films in English or with subtitles:

Cinéma Casino, Antibes
Boulevard du 24 Aout, 6-8.
Tel: 08 36 68 70 12.

Cinéma Les Arcades, Cannes
Rue Fèlix Faure, 77. Tel: 08 92 68 00 39.

Cinéma Sporting, Monaco
Place du Casino Monte-Carlo.
Tel: 08 36 68 00 72.

Cinématèque, Nice
Esplanade Kennedy 3. Tel: 04 92 04 06 66.

Cinéma Rialto, Nice
Rue de Rivoli, 4. Tel: 08 36 68 00 41.

Mercury, Nice
Place Garibaldi 16. Tel: 08 36 68 81 06.

Cabaret
The long-legged, sequin-adorned girls of the cabaret were made famous by artist Toulouse-Lautrec and it is still a singularly French form of entertainment. You can take in a show with dinner, or show only, at the following locations:

Le Baroque, near Nice
Avenue Pierre & Marie Curie, 06700 St Laurent-du-Var (just west of Nice). Tel: 04 93 31 54 97, www.lebaroque.fr

The Théâtre National hosts the Centre Dramatique National Nice Côte d'Azur

Le Cabaret du Casino, Monaco

This cabaret operates mid-Sept–Jun. *Monte-Carlo Casino, place du Casino. Tel: 377 93 50 69 31, www.montecarloresorts.com*

Salle des Etoiles, Monaco

This has a summer season (*Jun–mid-Sept*) of large-scale spectaculars. *Sporting Club of Monte-Carlo. Tel: 377 92 16 36 36.*

Casinos

There really was a man who broke the bank of Monte-Carlo, and the story has passed into popular legend. If you fancy your chances, then the Riviera is one of the best locations in the world to try your hand. The main venues are listed below, but there are also smaller casinos at Antibes, Juan-les-Pins, Cagnes-sur-Mer, Grasse and Menton.

Carlton Casino Club, Cannes

Boulevard Croisette 58. Tel: 04 92 99 51 00, www.partouche.fr

Casino de Monaco

Place du Casino. Tel: 377 93 50 69 31, www.montecarloresorts.com
The ornate gaming rooms are Grand Dame and the oldest in Europe but there are also excellent gaming rooms at Nice and Cannes.

Casino Rhul, Nice

Promenade des Anglais 1. Tel: 04 97 03 12 22.

PERFORMING ARTS

Two major auditoria along the Riviera act as magnets for major international acts and hold a varied programme of popular or classical music, ballet, jazz or opera. The finest are in Monaco and Nice.

Auditorium Rainier III

This is the home of the prestigious Monte-Carlo World Music awards each March. *Boulevard Louis II, 98004 Monaco. Tel: 377 93 10 85 00.*

Stade Nikaïa

The state-of-the-art auditorium and largest on the Riviera. If any international rock or pop performers play in the area, they will surely be booked in here. *Stade Charles Hermann, route de Grenoble, Nice. Tel: 08 20 02 04 06, www.nikaia.fr*

Many French cinemas show French and English language films

Theatre

The works of classical French bards such as Moliere or Hugo have stood the test of time and are still a regular part of any theatre programme. As with cinema, French theatre is still evolving, with several government-funded 'centres of excellence' throughout the country. The Centre Dramatique National Nice Côte d'Azur has developed into a major theatre company over the past few decades. Its home base is the Théâtre National but there are 11 other theatres in the city, each with a full programme. The theatre in Monaco, one of Princess Grace's own ideas, shows an eclectic mixture of performances.

Théâtre National de Nice
Promenade des Arts, Nice.
Tel: 04 93 13 90 90.

Théâtre Princess Grace, Monaco
Avenue d'Ostende 12, 98000 Monaco.
Tel: 377 93 50 03 45,
www.tpgmonaco.com

Opéra

Two opera companies have a home base on the Riviera. Opéra de Nice is at the opera house, whereas Opéra de Monte-Carlo performs at a number of different venues in Monaco.

Opéra de Nice
Rue St-François-de-Paule 4-6, Nice.
Tel: 04 92 17 40 79, www.ville-nice.fr

Opéra de Monte-Carlo
Place du Casino, 98000 Monaco.
Tel: 377 92 16 23 18, www.opera.mc

Ballet

The Ballet Corps of Monte-Carlo puts on a full programme throughout the year at its base.

Auditorium Rainier III
Boulevard Louis II, 98004 Monaco.
Tel: 377 92 16 24 06,
www.balletsdemontecarlo.mc

Music

Classical concerts have a host of memorable venues. The balmy summer evenings invite outdoor performances, from the Roman theatre at Fréjus to the majestic marble staircase of the Palais des Princes in Monaco. If you would prefer to be indoors, many historic churches hold summer concerts of chamber or choral music, using the acoustics of Romanesque, Gothic and Baroque naves and cupolas.

The Riviera's high-quality music festivals cover all styles. The Juan-les-Pins Jazz Festival is world renowned, while the Musical Nights of the Suquet in Cannes feature chamber music by new and established artists. In Nice, the unusual Vocalia polyphonic voice festival contrasts with the Pantiero contemporary music festival.

Music organisations based on the Riviera are the Orchestre Philarmonique de Monte-Carlo (*www.opmc.mc*) at Auditorium Rainier III, the Orchestre Philharmonique de Nice, which performs at various venues in the city (*Dec–Mar*) and the Choeur Philharmonique de Nice (*which both list their performances on www.nice-cotedazur.org*).

Children

Our What to See section has concentrated on the historical and cultural sites of the Riviera, which may be a turn-off for many children, but do not despair: this is most definitely a family destination.

Several amusement parks hold the promise of hours of fun

Beaches

The seaside is like a magnet to young children. With hundreds of beaches to choose from, it is a matter of finding one to suit your family's needs. In the resorts, beaches have cafés close by, some have trampolines and Juan-les-Pins has a small karting track. More remote beaches allow for exploration, particularly along the Esterel and Maures coasts. Beaches at Nice have pebbles, perfect for children who hate getting covered in sand, while St Tropez has fine golden sand.

Festivals and fairs

The festivals and fairs throughout the Riviera are perfect for children. Here there will be live music, costumed actors, merry-go-rounds and face-painting, not to mention delicious snacks when they get hungry. Many festivals, such as the Mardi-Gras in Nice, have colourful processions to watch; others have activities children can get involved in.

Kids' clubs

Three coastal towns offer France Station Nautique (water sports clubs for children) during the summer, with such activities as sailing, windsurfing and water-skiing. Children are divided by age and supervised by qualified staff.

Sessions, from 1 to 5 days, need to be booked in advance.
Cannes Jeunesse. Tel: 04 93 94 37 71, www.cannes.fr
Mandelieu-La Napoule. Tel: 04 93 49 95 31, www.ot-mandelieu.fr
Juan-les-Pins. Tel: 04 92 90 53 00, www.antibes-juanlespins.com

For younger children (ages 3–7) 'Mickey clubs' usually revolve around beach activities, but they are a great place for youngsters to socialise and perhaps speak a bit of French. They also allow parents to go and do some serious museum-bashing.

Le petit-train

Almost all the large towns and resorts have *petit-trains*. These are slow-moving, open carriages pulled by a tractor unit disguised as a train, and their guided itineraries take in the main museums and attractions. They are perfect for kids as they do not get tired and they get a better view than if they were walking through crowds of people.

Sports

The region has some of the most comprehensive sports facilities in Europe, with many English speaking instructors and a very high level of training and supervision, so if children want to try a new sport or simply enjoy one they are already proficient at – from horse riding to cycling, from windsurfing to snowboarding, this is the perfect place.

Theme parks

No, not quite Disney, but several large venues cater directly for children. There are huge waterparks with chutes, slides and wave-pools at Fréjus (Aquatica), Ste Maxime (Aqualand) and Antibes (Aquasplash).

Koalaland in Menton, Antibesland, and Lunapark at St Tropez are three fun-fairs with a range of rides for all ages (*details on www.azurpark.com*).

The zoo at Fréjus (*www.zoo-frejus.com*), the zoological park at St-Jean-Cap-Ferrat (*zoocapferrat.com*), village de Tortues and Marineland (*www.marineland.fr*), with its dolphin shows and butterfly jungle, all have a range of animals to enjoy.

You can also find adventure golf or mini-golf at several locations along the coast.

A disguise for a day keeps bad tempers at bay

Tips for a stress-free trip

Mix activities to keep their interest – boat trips between museums, parks between galleries. Try to alternate city with country days, or sightseeing with a day on the beach.

Take a favourite toy or colouring book to restaurants, so children have something to do between courses.

Substitute picnics for formal lunches, so you plan your own timing and menu.

And, if all else fails, France's famed pastries or ice creams will sooth temper tantrums for adults and children alike.

Sport and Leisure

Some of the most exciting Riviera sports cost nothing to watch; you simply take your place at the roadside or waterside to catch a glimpse of the action. For others, tickets are like gold-dust; unless you book well in advance, you will have to watch them on television in a local café.

The Riviera is well geared-up for two-wheeled traffic

Cycling

The famed Tour de France – probably the most popular free-to-view sporting competition in the world – wends its way around France during July each year. The route is published in October for the following year, and often includes stages along the Riviera (*see www.letour.fr*). However, there are always local races to bring the same sense of excitement, with hundreds of high-speed cyclists chasing through the countryside (*details at local tourist offices*).

Football/soccer

The emergence of the French national team in world football over the last 20 years reflects the competition in the French league, one of the most demanding in Europe. The Riviera has three strong teams, Monaco, Marseille and Nice.

Monaco
Stade Louis II, avenue des Castelans 7, Fontvielle. Tel: 377 92 05 40 11.

Olympic Marseille
Stade Vélodrome, rond-point de Prado, Marseille. Tel: 04 91 76 91 18.

OGC Nice
Stade du Ray, avenue du Ray 35, 06100 Nice. Tel: 04 92 07 06 06, www.ogcnice.com

Horse-racing

The Hippodrome de Côte d'Azur at Cagnes-sur-Mer is the only racecourse along the coast and it hosts flat-race (no jumps) cards between October and March.
Boulevard Kennedy 2, 06800 Cagnes-sur-Mer. Tel: 04 93 20 71 28.

Motor sport

The Monaco Grand Prix in May is without doubt the highlight of the Riviera's motor-sport calendar and the most glamorous weekend in Formula 1. The renowned Monte-Carlo Rally kicks the year off with white-knuckle racing around the hairpins of the *grande corniche* during January.

Powerboat racing

Sport of the super-rich, powerboat racing is expensive and dangerous, with speeds reaching over 150km/h (95mph). Monaco is the leading host along the Riviera, with competitions held throughout the summer.

Tennis

The Monte-Carlo Open is one of Europe's leading clay-court championships. As it takes place in late April, it is seen as final preparation for the summer Grand Slam season by its all-star start list.

Yachting

Dozens of regattas take place in the waters off the Riviera every year, where all classes of yachts compete for coveted awards. Without expert knowledge, it is difficult to keep abreast of who is actually leading the race, but the spectacle of hundreds of boats under full sail is breathtaking and the atmosphere in the ports is exhilarating.

PARTICIPATION SPORTS

The French have an almost feverish enthusiasm for sporting activities and claim to have invented several, including ballooning (Montgolfier brothers), flying (Blériot), SCUBA diving (Cousteau) and water-skiing (the lesser known Léo Roman).

You'll find safety and training standards are high, so if you want to learn a new sport this is a good place to do it.

Aerial sports

The climate of the Riviera is very conducive to taking to the air. For gliding (*vol à voile*), the centre of excellence is Fayence, but there are more than a dozen airfields where a variety of clubs meet to fly planes (*vol*), micro-lights (*ultra-léger motorisé*), hang-glide (*vol libre*) or launch themselves out of aeroplanes (*parachutisme*). These are privately-run members' clubs that generally welcome foreign members (though the price may be prohibitive for

Stade Louis II – home to Monaco's football team – sees capacity crowds on match days

short-term benefit, at about 200 euros) but they offer inexpensive introductions (*baptêmes*) for the beginner, at about 75 euros for a flight, 400 euros for parachute training and 230 euros for a tandem parachute jump.

Fédération Française de Vol Libre (www.ffvl.com) and Fédération Française Vol à Voile (www.ffvv.com) offer information on accredited organisations.

Parapente

The parapente is a little like a parachute, but more controllable, and you do not need an aircraft – a running jump from any high point launches you into the air! Pioneered in France, it is a hugely popular sport.

Take the plunge and go 'canyoning'

Parapente training courses cost about 400 euros, or try a tandem flight for 70 euros.

Fédération Française de Vol Libre (www.ffvl.com) has more information.

Canyoning

This relatively new sport (where participants scramble, swim and climb along river and stream courses) is already well established in the Riviera. The best sites are at St-Martin-Vésubie and in the Var tributaries. Always canyon with an accredited organisation on an accredited site.

Try Odyssée Verticale. Tel: 04 93 86 71 99, www.odyseeverticale.com

Climbing

The uplands provide opportunities for mountain climbing. The pre-Alps close to Nice, gorges at Verdon, and peaks in the Var are the best, but there are also six 'vertiginous hikes' already equipped with ropes, tethers and harnesses along the 'Via Ferrata' at Peille, Tende and other pre-Alps locations.

The Club Alpin de Français (*www.clubalpin.com*) has information about climbing schools and lessons, or equipment hire for experienced climbers. Prices for guides are about 300 euros per day, or 300 euros per person for a two-day group climb.

For climbing tuition or guiding contact Odyssée Verticale. Tel: 04 93 86 71 99, www.odyseeverticale.com

Cycling and mountain biking

Cycling is not just a serious sport here: *cyclisme* and *vélo tous terrains* (*VTT*) are also popular pastimes. As well as the

VTTs off road, summer weekends see large groups of cyclists on the roads, kitted out in full race colours. The Riviera has over 60 cycling itineraries for touring or day trips.

It is easy to rent bikes at resorts, and many railway stations also provide facilities (about 10 euros per day). *For cycle tours contact Sentiers d'Azur. Tel: 04 93 98 74 73, www.sentiersdazur.com*

Diving

Although the Mediterranean does not have the sea life of the Caribbean, there is still enough to make diving exciting, including shipwrecks from several eras. Excellent dive schools offer training to recognised standards, or accompanied dives if you are already qualified.

The CRT booklet 'Mer et Découverte' lists all diving schools in the region.

The Riviera has over 4,000km (250 miles) of marked footpaths

Golf

The Riviera is not awash with golf clubs, but you can take to the greens at eleven 18-hole courses. The course at Cannes-Mandelieu is said to be the third oldest in the world, founded in 1891. You can take to the course for 40 euros per round.

The regional tourism committee (CRT) produces a booklet 'Golf Destinations' with full details of courses in the region.

Kayaking/canoeing

All the gorges offer white-water experiences, but by their very nature these can be dangerous, so best travel with a guide. Sea kayaking is becoming more popular and you can rent equipment on site by the hour, the day or longer. You can take a day's group kayak ride for about 25 euros. *Fédération Française de Canöe-Kayak (www.ffck.org) is the national body. Aqua Viva Est organises tuition and guiding, April–Oct. Tel: 06 11 38 00 62, www.aquavivaest.com*

Riding

An exploration on four legs, or perhaps a little gymkhana practice, is available under the titles *randonnée équestre* and *équitation* respectively. A day's guided ride with picnic costs about 55 euros,

or about 20 euros an hour.
*Fédération Française d'Équitation
(www.ffe.com) has details of riding
establishments, as do local tourist offices.*

Sailing

The Riviera is a magnet for pleasure
sailing (*voile*), with excellent marina
facilities and a wide range of boats for
hire. You can take a boat with crew or,
if you have a skipper's certificate, 'bare'
(without crew). The largest ports for
yachts are at Antibes, Bandol, Cannes,
Hyères, St-Raphaël and Toulon, but
there are 37 in total with some
20,000 moorings. The regional tourism
committee (CRT) produces a booklet
'Mer et Découverte' listing all sailing
schools and pleasure ports in the region.

Offshore breezes offer perfect conditions for
windsurfing

Skiing/snowboarding

With the closest downhill station only
88km (55 miles) north of Nice, it is
easy to see how the city lives up to its
promise that you can ski in the morning
and swim in the sea in the afternoon.
Fifteen ski stations, including
international resorts Auron
(*www.auron.com*) and Isola 2000
(*www.isola2000.com*), lie in the
Mercantour National Park close to
its border with Italy.

Thalassothérapie

Not a sport, but the French invented
thalassothérapie or sea-water therapy,
which benefits the skin and (it is said)
numerous ailments. It is often used
in combination with other spa
treatments. There are ten centres in
the Riviera. They are listed in 'Mer
et Découverte'.

Walking and hiking (Randonnées pédestre)

France has over 30,000km (19,000 miles)
of footpaths, with a series of Grandes
Randonnées (long-distance footpaths)
and Petites Randonnées, which are
included on maps published by Institut
Geographique National (*Éspace IGN
rue la Boétie, 75008 Paris*).

The Riviera has over 4,000km (2,500
miles) of paths. Major ones are the GR5,
which starts at Nice and rises through
the Gorges de la Vésubie, the GR52,
linking the Vallée des Merveilles with
Sospel and Menton, and the GR52a,
which runs through the Col du Tende
and the Parc National du Mercantour.

To supplement this network,
départements and even local communes

have shorter walks mapped or signposted around lakes, along riverbanks or linking historical monuments. Most tourist offices along the Riviera have lots of information about footpaths and planned walks in their area.

For guided walks contact Alp'Azur Rando. Tel: 06 72 23 02 99, www.alpazurerando.free.fr

Windsurfing/Para-surfing

There are perfect conditions for these sports along the coast – particularly in the east of the region, with its wider bays. Renting boards costs from 20 euros an hour.

Information

Each commune in the Riviera has some form of sporting facility, be it a humble *boules* pitch, swimming pool (*piscine*) or tennis courts.

Information about all these facilities appears in local tourist information publications under *loisirs* (leisure).

Sea kayaking is fun for all ages

Boules

Aside from the rhythmical buzz of the cicada, the air of late afternoons on the Riviera is filled with the metallic clack of *boule* hitting *boule* as tournaments get under way under the shade of the plane or ash trees. This most French of games – seemingly a mixture of crown green bowls and marbles – is as much a part of life here as wine and olive oil.

This is no gentle pastime: players take even the most friendly game exceptionally seriously. It is often the place to sit and watch true Gallic spirit in the animated discussions that break out around close decisions or tactics gone awry.

How to play

Boules is a team game played on a *piste*, a hard surface at least 3m by 12m (10ft by 40ft). The game is made up of a number of 'ends' – with points being accumulated until one team has scored eleven.

Teams can number two people (*doublettes*) with three *boules* each, or three (*triplettes*) or four people (*quadrettes*) who have two *boules* each. The *boule* is a heavy metal-clad ball, large enough to sit in a cupped hand. Plastic boules are strictly for tourists and children!

The aim of the game is to get as many of your team's *boules* as close to the *cochonnet* (small marker ball) as possible. This can be achieved in two ways. Attackers (*pointeurs*) position their *boules* with precision, while defenders (*tireurs*) try to push the *boules* of the attackers aside, or off the *piste* altogether if possible. The classic attacking move is to position your ball so it is kissing the *cochonnet*. The classic defensive move is to hit the attacker's ball so that it flies out of the zone while yours takes its exact place – a very skilful manoeuvre requiring excellent hand–eye coordination.

There are two forms of the game. Where the jack is thrown over 10m (40ft), the game is *à la longue* and players take three hops before throwing or rolling the *boule*. Because space on *pistes* is normally at a premium, it is much more probable you will see the shorter game *à la pétanque* (sometimes

cochonnet wins one point for every boule which is closer than the closest opposing boule.

THE BEST PLACES TO WATCH BOULES

Place des Lices, St Tropez
La Place de Jeu, just outside the walls of
St Paul de Vence
Allées de la Liberté, by the port in Cannes

Opposite: A player patiently waits his turn
Above: The team with their boules closest to
the cochonnet wins
Below: Boules is a very sociable game

you will hear the game of boules referred to as pétanque because it is the standard form of the game), where the cochonnet is thrown closer to the players but they must make their play from a standing position without moving the feet. The name is derived from the phrase pieds tanqués ('feet together').

After the cochonnet is thrown, one player from each team throws one boule and the team with the ball furthest away from the cochonnet continue to throw until they have a boule closer than their opponents, or they have thrown all their boules. The opposing team then throw their boules, and the team with boule or boules closer to the

Food and Drink

Georges-Auguste Escoffier was born just west of Nice and his influence lives on in the outstanding restaurants of the region, managed by chefs as esteemed as artists. Food is not just sustenance here: it is treated with respect and reverence. The French demand the freshest ingredients and the highest expertise, so follow their lead and enjoy!

Where to eat? You will be spoiled for choice

When to eat

The French have quite a rigid eating schedule and most restaurants close between lunch and dinner. Lunch is generally the major meal of the day, served between noon and 2.30pm. Dinner starts about 7pm and serving finishes about 10pm, though in the hinterland they may close earlier, especially in winter.

Brasseries serve a limited menu (generally steaks, pasta and salads) throughout the day but you will find them only in cities and large towns.

Between meals, the French have a weakness for mouth-watering pastries (*pâtisserie*) or ice creams (*glâces*) and it is a delight to spend late afternoon in a café over one of these confections.

What to order

If you are on a budget, eat like the French and have your major meal at lunchtime (*déjeuner*). Most restaurants offer a set or limited-choice lunch menu at exceptional value. They will also have set menus for dinner (*dîner*) with a choice of two or three starters (*entrées*) and main courses (*plats*), with cheese (*fromages*) and a sweet course (*dessert*) included in the price. You can choose from the full menu (*à la carte*) if you prefer or if you want only one or two courses.

Brasseries and pizzerias have a less formal system; you can generally order from the menu.

Regional specialities

The coastal slopes, fragrant with wild herbs, were planted with olives by the ancient Greeks, and olive oil still dominates the menu. The warm days are conducive to growing fruit and vegetables – simply wandering past the market stalls of fat juicy tomatoes, courgettes and aubergines along with strong onions, peppers, artichokes and garlic is proof of that. The signature dish *ratatouille* (tomatoes, courgettes, aubergines and peppers, slow cooked in olive oil) makes the best of this fresh feast.

Meat has traditionally been tough beef or mutton from small herds and flocks that roamed free across the hillsides, so slow-cooked dishes called *estouffades* and *daubes* made the best of the cuts.

Along the coast, people grilled fish such as *rouget* (red mullet), *thon* (tuna), *loup* (sea bass) or *rascasse* (scorpion fish), together with *fruits de mer*, *langoustine* (crayfish), *huîtres* (oysters), *crevettes* (prawns), *moules* (mussels) and *homard* (lobster), or made *bouillabaisse*, a sort of fish stew (*see pp142–3*).

Closeness to Italy has resulted in some crossover of cuisine, with *pissaladière* being a close cousin of pizza, but made with onions, anchovies and black olives, while *pistou* is pesto. You also find gnocci and other pasta.

Speciality dishes

Tapenade – a paste of olives and anchovies often served on bread with aperitifs.
Brandade de morue – salt cod blended with garlic, oil and milk.
Salade Niçoise (salad of Nice) – tomatoes, beans, anchovies, olives, peppers and boiled eggs.
Pain bagnat (literally 'soaked bread') – a roll softened with olive oil and garlic, containing salad, anchovies and olives.
Porchetta – stuffed roasted suckling pig.
Salade de Mesclun – a green salad made with a mixture of local leaves.

Ordering meat

The French enjoy lightly cooked meat and there may be raised eyebrows if you order yours well done, but stand your ground! Here are phrases you will need.
saignant – bloody in the centre.
bleu – rare in the centre.
à point – brown but with the narrowest pink line in the centre.
plus à point – brown throughout.
bien cuit – dark brown exterior, cooked through.

Drinks

Because of the hot, dry climate, local wines are no match for Burgundy or Bordeaux, but their lighter, fruitier flavours do make perfect accompaniments to your alfresco meals or simply to drink on the terrace – particularly the *rosés (see p67)*.

The other major drink of the south is *pastis*, an aniseed aperitif, which is diluted with water. Proprietary brands include Ricard and Pastis 51.

Shopping for food

Buying food, for picnics or to take home, is a delight. You can purchase wine, olive oil, honey, jams, wild herbs, cheese and strings of garlic direct from the producers (*see pp170–71*) as you are touring in the hills.

Shopping in France centres on the High Street, where you will find a range of specialist, usually family owned, establishments. Head to the *boulangerie* for bread, *pâtisserie* for pastries, *boucherie* for meat, *charcuterie* for cooked meats and pâtés, *fromagerie* for cheese and, if you need a general store, look for the word *alimentation*.

Hypermarkets (*hypermarchés*) bring self-service shopping to France. Standards are high and the best (*Leclerc, Carrefour, Champion, Super U*) will offer food from across the country. You will normally find hypermarkets at the *centre commercial*. This will be well signposted.

Restaurants

Prices can vary widely in restaurants and these should only be used as a rough guide:

*	Under €30
**	€30–€46
***	€46–€76
****	Over €76

Auberge de la Madone***
Pretty terrace at this renowned family
owned auberge/hotel at the entrance
to Peillon village.
06440 Peillon. Tel: 04 93 79 91 17.

Auberge des Seigneurs**
Medieval auberge that specialises in spit
roasted meats.
Place Frêne, 06570 Vence.
Tel: 04 93 58 04 24.

Auberge St Pierre**
18th-century hotel/restaurant, with
Escoffier-trained chef producing varied
menu with local ingredients.
Route d'Ampus, 83690 Tourtour.
Tel: 04 94 70 59 04.

Auberge du Vieux Château**
Small family-owned Provençal restaurant
with panoramic views from the terrace.
Place du Panorama, 06530 Cabris.
Tel: 04 93 60 50 12.

La Bergerie***
Excellent rustic local cuisine with
panoramic views.
Grand Corniche, Col d'Eze.
Tel: 04 93 41 03 67.

Le Chantclar****
Long-established restaurant with
traditional haute-cuisine menu.
Promenade des Anglais 37, 06000 Nice.
Tel: 04 93 88 39 51.

La Chèvre d'Or****
A gastronomic menu with exhilarating
views, perched above the coast.
Rue du Barri, 06360 Eze. Tel: 04 92 10 66 66.

Le Cosi***
Stylish bistro with tables on the main
street through le Suquet for atmospheric
summer dinners.

Rue du Suquet 10-14, 06400 Cannes.
Tel: 04 93 68 66 79, www.lecosi.com

Les Deux Frères**
On the edge of the village, with
exceptional views of the coastline
below from the dining terrace.
06190 Roquebrune-Cap-Martin.
Tel: 04 93 28 99 00.

Galeries des Arcades**
Traditional dishes with local ingredients
in the historic place des Arcades.
Place des Arcades 16, 06410 Biot.
Tel: 04 93 65 01 04.

Hôtel des Deux Rocs**
Simple but delicious menu and rustic
tables outside under the plane trees.
Place font d'Amout, 83440 Seillans.
Tel: 04 94 76 87 32.

Le Logis du Guetteur***
Views down over the village from the
terrace, or eat in the medieval dining
room. Several menus to choose from.
Place du Château, 83460 les Arcs-sur-
Argens. Tel: 04 94 99 51 10.

Le Louis XV****
The only 6-star Michelin restaurant in
the world, with an exquisite and inventive
menu plus exceptional wine list.
Hôtel de Paris, place du Casino, MC
98000 Monaco. Tel: (377) 92 16 29 76.

La Mère Germaine**
Atmospheric terrace on the quayside of
the town, menu concentrates on seafood.
Quai Courbet, 06230 Villefranche-sur-Mer.

Le Moulin de Mougins****
Chef Roger Vergé's Michelin star-rated
cuisine attracts gourmets, the famous
and the wealthy.
Quartier Notre-Dame-de-Vie, 06250
Mougins. Tel: 04 93 75 78 24.

Nissa Socca*
Traditional socca (chickpea flour pancake) with plates of pasta and carafes of wine.
Rue Sainte-Réparate 5, 06000 Nice. Tel: 04 93 80 18 35.

Restaurant l'Oasis****
The most renowned restaurant on this part of the coast.
Rue Jean-Honoré-Carle 6, 06210 La Napoule. Tel: 04 93 49 95 52.

Ristorante Galerie d'Art d'Angelina**
An eclectic but atmospheric modern bistro/art gallery.
Avenue Victor Hugo 7, 13260 Cassis. Tel: 04 42 01 89 27.

Royal Gray**
Grand-Dame of Cannes restaurants.
Rue des Serbes 38, 06400 Cannes. Tel: 04 92 99 79 60.

L'Univers de Christian Plumail***
Modern city-centre restaurant where the chef concentrates on local ingredients.
Boulevard Jean Jaurès 54, 06300 Nice. Tel: 04 93 62 32 22.

Bars
L'Amiral
Where anyone who is anyone comes for an early evening drink.
The Martinez Hôtel, boulevard de la Croisette 73, 06400 Cannes. Tel: 04 92 98 73 00.

Café de Paris
The most fashionable bar along the St Tropez quayside. Sit and watch the world go by.
Quai de Suffren, 83990 St Tropez. Tel: 04 94 97 00 56.

Café de Paris
Meeting place of the 'beautiful people'.
Hôtel de Paris, Place du Casino, 98001 Monte-Carlo. Tel: 377 92 16 25 25.

La Terrasse
Exceptional views over the harbour and superb cocktails are the draw here.
Place Beaumarchais, 98001 Monte-Carlo. Tel: 377 92 16 40 00.

Les Trois Diables
The liveliest bar amongst several that make Cours Selaya as busy in the evening as it is during the day.
Cours Selaya 2, 06000 Nice. Tel: 04 93 62 47 00.

Food
Alziari
A selection of the region's best olive oil and other regional products.
Rue St François de Paule 14, 06000 Nice. Tel: 04 93 85 76 92.

Balade en Provence
Full range of olive oils and Provençal foodstuffs, exceptional range of *anis* drinks (also in Nice).
Marché Provençal, Cours Masséna 25, 06600 Antibes. Tel: 04 93 34 93 00.

Confiseries Florian
Store at factory producing jam, crystallised flowers and fruit, jelly sweets and candy (also in Nice).
Pont-du-Loup, 06140 Tourrettes-sur-Loup. Tel: 04 93 59 32 91.

Moulin de Callas
Olive grove and mill, selling oils, soaps, jams and olive wood products.
Quartier les Ferrages, 83830 Callas (near Draguignan). Tel: 04 94 76 68 05.

Olivier & Cie.
Olive oils from around the Mediterranean and tapenade, taste and buy (also at Nice, Antibes and St Tropez).
Rue Macé 4, 06400 Cannes. Tel: 04 93 39 00 38.

The French Market

Where we tend to find shopping is a chore to be fitted into our hectic lives – even a dreaded necessity before the fun can begin – *le marché*, the French market, is an event to be savoured, a must-have experience even if you do not intend to buy anything.

Markets are a French institution, particularly their produce markets. They still form an essential part of rural life, despite the arrival of supermarkets and hypermarkets and there are two main reasons for this. Firstly, the quality of the produce on sale is first-class. Local producers of meats, cheeses, fruit and vegetables know their produce inside out and their pride in their work can be seen in the way they display their wares from hand-tied bundles of asparagus to straw-wrapped cheese. You know that everything sold is fresh, even perhaps picked that very morning.

Markets are also the place to find the local produce that cannot be exported because of EC rules, delicious cheeses made from non-pasteurised milk for instance, or pâtés produced without certain preservatives. Foodstuffs such as this have been produced for centuries, but can now be sold only in their place of origin.

The second reason for the continued health of the market is that it is a social event for the local community. It is a chance to take a morning away from the farm or vineyard and meet your friends, to exchange ideas, political arguments or family news. A trip to the market always includes an hour or so at the local café, perhaps even an alfresco lunch. For

visitors it is a great place to people-watch, because everyone comes here to shop – from the wife of the local mayor, dressed in a classic suit, to the farmers in berets and boots. Merchandise is stored away in chic designer bags or straw panniers, carried home in a top-of-the-range Renault or the basket of an old bicycle.

For the French, shopping is an art form. One strolls and peruses. One rubs one's chin, perhaps picking up an article and asking questions about it. One makes an active choice. All attention is given to the produce. Do not be shy about asking to taste what you are buying: it is quite a normal part of *marché* shopping.

Opposite: Browsing for *brocantes* – the perfect way to spend the afternoon
Above: Tempting fresh produce is a trademark of a French market

DIFFERENT TYPES OF MARKET

Brocantes – articles somewhere between flea market junk and genuine antiques.

Vide Greniers – literally 'empty attics', this market is a little like a car-boot sale, when people sell on their unwanted goods.

Marché aux Puces – flea market, where you can find anything and everything.

The best markets in the Riviera are at the Cours Saleya in Nice, Cours Masséna in Antibes and the Cours Lafayette in Toulon. In all these places markets are held daily from Tuesday to Saturday and on Sunday morning. There are often smaller markets and antiques markets in Riviera towns.

See the local *Mairie* (town hall) for details.

Most of us do not live the jet-set lifestyle but we would like to give it a try, even if only for a week or so. So how do the beautiful people while away their time on the Riviera. What would the ultimate trip be?

Firstly, you would need to plan your trip around the time when everyone-who-is-anyone is also here – try the Monaco Grand Prix on Ascension Day weekend, or Cannes Film Festival in mid-May.

Next, you will need to think about somewhere to stay. Only certain hotels will fit the bill: a luxury bolt-hole in a medieval village, such as the Château Eza (until 1953 the home of one of the Swedish royal family), or a suite at a *belle époque* Grand Dame – think the Carlton in Cannes, Negresco in Nice or Hôtel de Paris in Monte-Carlo – so you are only a stone's-throw from the action.

Many celebrities prefer not to mix with hoi polloi and find it easier to relax in a villa or on a boat – a floating gin-palace is kitted out with more luxury than any hotel room and has enough cabins to accommodate 15 people comfortably. Do not think about lifting a finger, because you will have staff to cater to your every whim – so no cooking, cleaning or making the evening cocktails!

Once you have settled in, you will need to plan your itinerary. Museums and other attractions are down to personal taste but, apart from the day's touring, there are some activities and establishments that you cannot leave off the list.

Lunch – to be seen, you will need to be at a beachfront restaurant and that

Valdrôme

means Cannes or, better still, Club 55 at St Tropez – take a table in a prime position to watch the world go by.

Aperitifs need to be taken along the quayside at St Tropez, where it is not so much the particular bar, but the position on the front row nearest the port, which is important, or the Café de Paris in Monte-Carlo, then on to dinner at one of the Michelin star establishments – the best being Le Louis XV at the same hotel.

Finish off the evening at a nightclub. Jimmy'z in Monte-Carlo is legendary for the smart set (you will really need to dress up for this – maybe do some shopping while you are there) or Les Caves du Roy in St Tropez – very exclusive but a little more relaxed. Or head to the casino to take a chance amongst the high-rollers.

And here is a draft budget to give you pause for thought.

A week's rental of a 12m (40ft) motor-boat, from 9,750 euros, a 35m (115ft) boat with crew, from 97,300 euros, plus $1/3$ of this sum for fuel, food and other consumables.

Villa rental with staff, from 4,000 euros per week – larger villas on, say, Cap Ferrat or Cap-Martin, from 20,000 euros per week.

Rental of a decent car (Porsche or Ferrari), from 500 euros per day.

Suite at Château Eza in Eze, from 730 euros per night.

Meal at the Le Louis XV, 300 euros per person.

Outfit from Dior, about 2,000 euros.

Admission into the gaming rooms of the Monte-Carlo casino, a snip at 20 euros.

Opposite: A life on the ocean wave – hiring a yacht is easy
Above: Villa rental offices offer a first class service
Below: Attentive waiters cater to your every need

Hotels and Accommodation

The Riviera offers some of the most luxurious accommodation in the world. Yet it is still possible to enjoy a good standard even if you are on a budget, especially early or late in the season. Every tourist office keeps a comprehensive list of accommodation in their area.

Luxury hotels like the Carlton in Cannes can also be historic landmarks

Hotels

The Riviera has a good selection of hotels in all price ranges, with a wealth of choice in the upper price and quality ranges. One-third of the hotels are rated at 4 or 5 stars. In most hotels there will be a range of room sizes and standards that vary in price (you will pay extra for a sea-view or balcony), so do make sure that you are specific in your demands when enquiring or booking. In the lower star-rated hotels, bathrooms can be small: ask about size before booking. Room prices also vary with the season, being most expensive between mid-July and the end of August.

Breakfast is rarely included in the room price. Continental breakfast (coffee, bread, croissant/brioche and jam) is usually over-priced in hotels. It is much cheaper and more atmospheric to take breakfast at a local café.

Villa rental

Self-catering accommodation ranges from tiny studios to ten-bedroom houses with swimming pools or jacuzzis. It really depends on your budget and where you want to base yourself. Prices start from about 400 euros per week in peak season. Country properties for rent are known as *gîtes*.

Gîtes de France is the national organisation; its local office is at *promenade des Anglais 57, B.P. 1602, 06011 Nice. Tel: 04 92 15 21 30, www.guideriviera.com/gites06*

Boat hire

Making your holiday water-based instead of land-based is easy and practical on the Riviera (though not necessarily a budget option!). During peak season it is probably easier to travel from port to port by boat than by road, or you could anchor offshore to avoid the hustle and bustle. Rental prices start from about 12,000 euros per week in peak season.

Camping

Campsites are common from Toulon to just west of Nice, but non-existent along the corniches in the far east of the region. You can find sites directly on the seafront or deep inland surrounded by fragrant forest or hectares of vines. The regional tourist office (CRT) produces a booklet on camping throughout the Côte d'Azur, and each commune or major resort will have a list of accredited sites locally.

Chambres d'hôte

The French equivalent of 'bed and breakfast' has been growing in popularity over the last decade and you will find rooms in farmhouses, villas and even historic châteaux. Standards are similarly varied. Not all tourist offices keep lists of *chambres d'hôte*, though some have a rating system. As you travel, look for signs outside properties if they have vacancies.

A word of warning

All forms of accommodation in all price ranges are under pressure during the French summer holidays, between mid-July and the end of August. If you intend to stay in the Riviera then, it is vital to make a firm booking in advance, to avoid disappointment.

SUGGESTED HOTELS
Prices

The guide prices here are based on a typical double room per night, including tax but not usually breakfast.

Simple rooms in the centre of St Tropez

Budget (under 100 euros)
Hôtel Agata

Modern comfortable if bland hotel, good for city stays (45 rooms).
Boulevard Carnot 46, 06300 Nice.
Tel: 04 93 55 97 13,
www.agatahotel.com

Hôtel le Baron

Set at the top of St Tropez old town, the hotel has a bar and restaurant (10 rooms).
Rue de l'Aïoli 23, 83990 St Tropez.
Tel: 04 94 97 06 57.

Hôtel Beau Soleil

Modern hotel with pool and car park 500m from the beach (30 rooms).
Impasse Beau Soleil, 06220 Golfe-Juan.
Tel: 04 93 63 63 63,
www.hotel-beau-soleil.com

Hôtel Clair Logis

Small hotel in the heart of town (18 rooms).
Avenue Central 12, 06230 St Jean-Cap-Ferrat. Tel: 04 93 76 51 81,
www.hotel-clair-logis.fr

Les Deux Frères

Small hotel at the entrance to Roquebrune village. Restaurant terrace with panoramic views (10 rooms).
06190 Roquebrune-Cap-Martin.
Tel: 04 93 28 99 00,
www.lesdeuxfreres.com

Hôtel le Golfe

Located on the Cassis harbour front with some rooms overlooking the port (30 rooms).
Place du Grand Carnot 3, Quai Barthélémy,
13260 Cassis. Tel: 04 42 01 00 21.

L'Horizon

Provençal mansion with panoramic views set in the foothills behind Cannes (22 rooms).

A room with a view over the harbour at Cassis

Promenade Saint-Jean 100, 06530 Cabris-Grasse. Tel: 04 93 60 51 69.

Hôtel Marc Hély

Farmhouse style hotel inland from the Baie des Anges between Cannes and Nice (12 rooms).
Route de Cagnes 535, 06480 La Colle-sur-Loup. Tel: 04 93 22 64 10.

Hôtel de Londres

Small mansion on the main approach road into the town (26 rooms).
Avenue Carnot 15, 06502 Menton. Tel: 04 93 35 74 62, www.hotel-de-londres.com

Les Trois Vallées

Mountain lodge on the edge of the Parc de Mercantour (20 rooms).
Col du Turini, 06440 Turini. Tel: 04 93 91 57 21.

Standard (100–200 euros)

Auberge du Petit Palais

Belle-époque hotel in the heart of the Cimiez residential area close to the Roman remains (25 rooms).
Avenue Emile Bieckert 17, 06000 Nice.

Tel: 04 93 62 19 11, www.guide-gerard.com

La Bastide de Tourtour

Large stone 'bastide' surrounded by exceptional countryside (25 rooms).
Route de Flaysoc, 83690 Tourtour. Tel: 04 98 10 54 20.

La Grande Bastide

Eighteenth-century fortified mansion with views across the village. Individually decorated rooms. Pool and terrace (11 rooms).
Route de la Colle, 06570 St-Paul-de-Vence. Tel: 04 93 32 50 30.

Hostellerie Le Baou

Quiet retreat with view over the Maures woodland to the St Tropez beaches, excellent restaurant (39 rooms).
Avenue Gustave Etienne, 83350 Ramatuelle. Tel: 04 98 12 94 20.

Hôtel Golfe de Valescure

Modern hotel set around a pine-clad golf course. All rooms have terrace (40 rooms).
Avenue Paul l'Hermite, 83700 Saint-Raphaël. Tel: 04 94 52 85 00.

Hôtel de Paris

Flamboyant *belle-époque* mansion situated 500m from the Croisette and the beach. Swimming pool (50 rooms).
Boulevard d'Alsace 34, 06400 Cannes. Tel: 04 97 06 98 80.

Hôtel Sainte-Valérie

Beautiful mansion in the heart of the resort (25 rooms).
Rue de l'Oratoire, 06160 Juan-les-Pins. Tel: 04 93 61 07 15.

La Maurette Roquebrune

Stone *mas* with rustic furnishings perched on a hillside. Pool (11 rooms).
La Maurette, 83520 Roquebrune-sur-Argens. Tel: 04 98 11 43 53.

Relais Cantemerle
Rooms set in verdant gardens 2km from St Paul (20 rooms).
Chemin Cantemerle 258, 06140 Vence. Tel: 04 93 58 08 18, www.relais-cantemerle.com.

Villa Mauresque
Moorish villa designed by Chaploulard in 1760 set in tropical gardens just outside St-Raphaël (7 rooms).
Route de la Corniche 1792, 83700 Boulouris. Tel: 04 94 83 02 42.

Luxury (over 200 euros)

Les Bories
Bungalows built in the style of traditional shepherds' huts set amongst the maquis. Health and fitness centre (26 rooms).
Route de l'Abbaye de Sénanque, 84220 Gordes. Tel: 04 90 72 00 51.

Le Cagnard
Thirteenth-century fortified mansion with exquisitely decorated rooms and suites (20 rooms).
Rue Sous Barri, Haut-de-Cagnes, 06800 Cagnes-sur-Mer. Tel: 04 93 20 73 21.

Château Eza
Set atop the medieval village of Eze, this was once a royal residence (10 rooms).
Rue de la Pise, 06360 Eze. Tel: 04 93 41 12 24.

La Colombe d'Or
The café to a generation of 20th century artists is now a sumptuous hotel for its up-market 21st century clientele (25 rooms).
Place de Gaulle, 06570 St Paul-de-Vence. Tel: 04 93 32 80 02.

Hôtel Île Rousse
Set on a sandy bay with watersports centre and four restaurants (52 rooms).

Boulevard Louis Lumière 25, 83150 Bandol. Tel: 04 94 29 33 00.

Les Mas Candille
House set in 4 hectares of Provençal parkland and olive groves (39 rooms).
Boulevard Clément Rebuffel, 06250 Mougins. Tel: 04 92 28 43 43.

Monte-Carlo Beach Hotel
1930s' hotel on a splendid bay with pines, beach and azure water (41 rooms).
Avenue Princess Grace, 06190 Roquebrune-Cap-Martin. Tel: 04 93 28 66 66.

Hôtel le Negresco
The most famous hotel along the Riviera this *belle-époque* jewel is still the height of luxury (143 rooms).
Promenade des Anglais 37, 06000 Nice. Tel: 04 93 88 39 51.

La Réserve de Beaulieu
Elegance is the watchword of this coastal Florentine mansion with spa and private harbour (27 rooms).
Boulevard du Général Leclerc 5, 06310 Beaulieu-sur-Mer. Tel: 04 93 01 00 01.

Many hotels feature shady terraces

Practical Guide

Arriving
Entry formalities

Nationals from most EU countries need only an identity card to enter France and may stay for up to three months. UK citizens need a passport, as do citizens of the US, Canada and New Zealand, and may stay for up to three months.

Australian citizens require a passport and tourist visa to enter France. This is obtained from the French Embassy in Australia before departure.

For other non-EU nationals, consult the French Embassy in your own country.

Arriving by air

The major airport of entry is Nice-Côte d'Azur, which accepts flights from Paris and other French cities, and numerous direct international flights. There are bus services to Nice Airport from Monaco and Cannes.
Nice-Côte d'Azur Airport.
Tel: 0820 423 333 (within France),
www.nice.aeroport.fr

There is also an international airport at Marseille and domestic airports at Toulon-Hyères (*Tel: 04 94 00 83 83, www.adth.fr*), Cannes-Mandelieu (*Tel: 08 20 42 66 66, www.cannes-mandelieu.aeroport.fr*), and the private charter airport at St Tropez-La Mole (*Tel: 04 94 54 76 54, www.st-tropez-airport.com*).

Arriving by rail

The *Train à Grande Vitesse* (*TGV*) or High-Speed Train is the backbone of the French Railway system and the envy of most of Europe for its fast and efficient service. From Paris (Gare du Lyon) it is 5 hours to Nice.
French Railways (SNCF).
Tel: 08 36 35 35 39, www.sncf.fr

Arriving by road

France's excellent motorway system of *autoroutes à péage* offers easy access to the Riviera from the north and west. This is a toll network with a good number of service stations (*aires de service*) and rest areas (*aires*).

The main non-toll roads, 'N' roads, are also generally of good quality but will route you through major towns and cities and thus are slower.

OFFICE DE TOURISME

Look for this sign for tourist information

The Riviera has a choice of commercial airports

Arriving by coach

Eurolines (*www.eurolines.fr*) has a cross-Europe network with over 1,500 destinations. The drop-off and pick-up points in the Riviera are St Raphaël, Nice, Cannes and Hyères, though the nearest ticket office is in Marseille. Journey times can be long and some routes may involve transfers to reach your destination.

Camping

Campsites are of a good standard and are numerous along the coast from Nice to Marseille. Sites are graded with a star system similar to that of hotels, with four stars being the best equipped. Most campsites are open May–Sept, few being open all year. It is essential to make a reservation if you wish to visit between mid-July and the end of August as almost all sites will be fully booked.

Children

The Riviera has excellent recreation facilities for children, with reduced admission at most attractions and on public transport.

More and more restaurants offer children's menus and child-sized portions but owners and fellow patrons will expect children to be well behaved.

If you travel with children during the summer, make sure you adequately protect them against the strong sun. In some parts of the coast, mosquitoes may be a problem so take insect repellent.

Climate

The Riviera has a mild temperate climate with hot, dry summers, wet springs and autumns, and cool winters. Frost and snow are rare phenomena. The best times to visit are late May–June and September when the temperatures are pleasant for both sightseeing and beach activities.

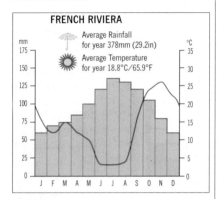

FRENCH RIVIERA

Average Rainfall for year 378mm (29.2in)

Average Temperature for year 18.8°C/65.9°F

Weather Conversion Chart
25.4mm = 1 inch
°F = 1.8 × °C + 32

Crime

If you visit the Riviera, you will be at a relatively low risk of being a victim of serious crime, but 'petty crime' such as theft is a problem, so take the following precautions:

- do not leave valuables in a car and leave nothing on show
- do not carry large amounts of cash or valuables with you
- deposit valuables in the hotel safe
- take extra care at cash-point machines
- carry handbags over your shoulder and across your chest to thwart bag-snatchers
- do not leave valuables unattended on the beach or in cafés/restaurants

Customs regulations

EU citizens can bring unlimited amounts of duty-payable goods for their own use if they travel from another EU country.

Non-EU citizens, and EU citizens arriving in France from a non-EU country, may bring the following amounts of duty-payable goods duty-free:

- 400 cigarettes, plus 50 cigars or 50g tobacco
- 2 litres wine and 1 litre liqueur/spirits
- half-litre of perfume

Driving

The French drive on the right and overtake on the left, with priority given to those on the major route unless otherwise posted. On roundabouts, traffic already on the roundabout has priority.

Traffic in the Riviera is heavy, especially in the cities, so allow plenty of time for journeys. Signposting is not always good, with some signs being just on the junction rather than well before it. One-way systems can cause problems for non-residents; bus lanes are common.

General rules include: seatbelts must be worn, children under 10 must travel on the back seat, the blood alcohol limit is 0.50g/litre, and you must carry your car documents and driving licence with you. There are on-the-spot fines for speeding and drink-driving.

In general, roads in France are of good quality. Motorways (A roads) are toll roads (*autoroutes à péage*). *Routes nationales* (RN or N roads) are arterial routes and *routes départementales* (D roads) are secondary routes.

Roads signposted *Bis* are cross-country, secondary routes linking major cities that circumvent crowded routes.

Standard speed limits are: on *autoroutes*, 130km/h (80mph) in dry weather, 110km/h (70mph) in the wet; on dual carriageways, 110km/h in the dry weather, 100km/h (62mph) in the wet; on other routes, 90km/h (55mph) in dry and 80km/h (50mph) in wet weather; and in towns 50km/h (30mph).

If you break down, place a red warning triangle behind your car and put on your hazard warning lights. *Autoroutes* have emergency telephones where you can arrange for help. If you are driving your own car, it is advisable to have breakdown cover with a reputable company.

Street parking is restricted; parking in cities and along the coast can be in short supply. However, car parks (usually 'pay and display') are well signposted and numerous.

Most of the medieval hill villages allow only local traffic, so use the car parks provided and enter on foot.

To fill up with petrol (gas), look for *essence*, usually *sans plomb* (without lead); for diesel, you want *gasoil*. Most garages are self-service, open 24 hours, with pumps operated by credit card.

All the major car rental companies have offices in the Riviera and it is easy to pick up a car at the major airports. Prices are relatively expensive. You will need a full driver's licence and to be over 21 (some companies say 23 or 25).

Electricity

France operates on 220 volts. Plugs have either two or three round pins. Visitors will need adaptors to use electrical equipment, and travellers from North America will need a power converter (transformer).

The perfect camping spot – right on the beach!

Embassies

All foreign embassies are in Paris.
Some countries also have consular
services in cities along the Riviera
(*see list below*).

USA

Embassy: avenue Gabriel 2, 75008 Paris.
Tel: 01 43 12 22 22.
Consulate: avenue Gustav V 7, Nice.
Tel: 04 93 88 89 55.

UK

Embassy: rue du Faubourg St-Honoré,
75008 Paris. Tel: 01 44 51 31 00.
Consulate General: avenue du Prado 24,
Marseille. Tel: 04 91 15 72 10.
Consulate: avenue Notre Dame 26, Nice.
Tel: 04 93 62 13 56.

Canada

Embassy: avenue Montagne 35, 75008
Paris. Tel: 01 44 43 29 00.
Consulate: rue Lamartine, Nice.
Tel: 04 93 92 93 22.

Ireland

Embassy: rue Rude 4, 75016 Paris.
Tel: 01 44 17 67 00.
Consulate General: boulevard
J F Kennedy 152, Cap d'Antibes.
Tel: 04 93 61 50 63.

Australia

Embassy: rue Jean Rey 4, 75015 Paris.
Tel: 01 40 59 33 00.

New Zealand

Embassy: rue Léonard da Vinci 7, 75016
Paris. Tel: 01 45 01 43 43.

Emergency

The following telephone numbers are
national freephone numbers.

17 – police
18 – Sapeurs Pompiers for fire or crash
rescue
15 – SAMU paramedics

Health

The French health system is regarded as
one of the finest in the world and the
quality of care is excellent.

For EU citizens most treatment costs
will be refunded but you must carry a
valid E111 form signed and dated at
your local post office. If you visit a
doctor, you will receive a bill for the
consultation and for the treatment (this
is standard for French citizens also),
which you pay immediately. The money
can then be claimed back from your
national social services agency or from
your insurance company (*see Insurance,*
below).

Non-EU citizens will be charged for
all treatment and should have adequate
insurance cover (*see Insurance, below*).

Pharmacies

For minor ailments (coughs, colds,
stomach aches) visit a pharmacy or
chemist (indicated by green cross sign)
where the pharmacist is qualified to
advise (without charge) and dispense
treatment for a variety of health
problems. Many drugs sold in
supermarkets in the UK (such as aspirin
or cough syrup) can be bought only in a
pharmacy in France.

Insurance

Having adequate insurance cover is vital.

Travellers should have cover for
everything they carry with them –
clothing, valuables and cash – in case
of loss or theft.

Non-EU citizens should ensure that
they have adequate health insurance to
cover illness or injury. This can also
include repatriation in the event of a

serious injury or illness. EU citizens may also wish to take out such cover, as the E111 form will mean treatment is free in France, but it won't make arrangements for you to travel home in the event of injury or illness.

Insurance companies also usually provide cover for cancellation or travel delay in their policies. Though not essential cover, this offers some compensation when travel plans go awry.

Lost property

Airports and railway stations have lost-property departments, or try the local police station. You will need an official police report to make an insurance claim for any lost property. If you lose your passport, contact your embassy or consulate immediately.

Maps

Michelin produce maps (*cartes*) of extremely high quality, perfect for touring and available at bookshops and motorway service stations. Most tourist offices produce a free map (*plan*) of their town or city with enough detail to locate museums and other attractions.

Media

France has a range of daily newspapers reflecting the political spectrum, including *Le Figaro* and *Le Monde*. The main local daily is *Nice-Matin*. *The European* (weekly) presents a pan-European perspective in English and the *International Herald Tribune* (daily) reports international news from a US standpoint. Both are widely available. It is possible to buy all the main British dailies.

Money matters
Money

France uses the euro (€) as currency. Each euro is divided into 100 cents. Notes are worth 5, 10, 50, 100, 200 or 500 euros, each a different size and colour. Coins come in values of 1, 2, 10, 20 and 50 cents, and 1 or 2 euros.

Banks and official exchange bureaux (*bureaux de change*) will change money (you will need your passport for identification) but it is much more efficient to use an international debit card to take euros out of your account through an ATM or cash-point machine, using your own 4-digit PIN number.

Scooters are a popular mode of transport

LANGUAGE

PRONUNCIATION

French words are unstressed, meaning that equal emphasis is given to each syllable.

Understanding the pronunciation of the following vowels or groups of vowels will help you to speak better French:

a	ah	**ei**	eh	
ai	eh	**i**	ee	
au	oh	**o**	oh	
e	ee	**ou**	oo	
eu	uh	**oi**	wah	

All French objects are either male or female. Male objects are referred to as *le* (such as *le bateau*, the boat) or *un* (*un bateau*, a/one boat), whilst female objects are referred to as *la* (*la voiture*, the car) or *une* (*une voiture*, a/one car).

NUMBERS		DAYS OF THE WEEK		MONTHS	
one	un, une	**Monday**	lundi	**January**	janvier
two	deux	**Tuesday**	mardi	**February**	février
three	trois	**Wednesday**	mercredi	**March**	mars
four	quatre	**Thursday**	jeudi	**April**	avril
five	cinq	**Friday**	vendredi	**May**	mai
six	six	**Saturday**	samedi	**June**	juin
seven	sept	**Sunday**	dimanche	**July**	juillet
eight	huit			**August**	août
nine	neuf			**September**	septembre
ten	dix			**October**	octobre
one hundred	cent			**November**	novembre
				December	décembre

USEFUL PHRASES

Do you speak English?	Parlez-vous anglais?
I don't understand	Je ne comprends pas
Where is/are?	Où est/sont?
Could you speak less quickly?	Pouvez-vous parler moins vite?
Please	S'il vous plaît
Thank you	Merci
Excuse me	Excusez-moi
What is your name?	Comment-vous appelez-vous?
My name is	Je m'appelle ...
I would like	Je voudrais ...
How much does this cost?	C'est combien?
What time is it?	Quelle heure est-il?

GENERAL				
yes	oui	**ahead**	tout droit
no	non	**closed**	fermé, fermée
large	grand, grande	**entrance**	l'entrée
small	petit, petite	**exit**	la sortie
left	gauche	**when?**	quand?
right	droite	**what?**	quel? quelle?
open	ouvert, ouverte		

Credit cards

Credit cards are widely accepted in shops, restaurants and hotels. French credit cards are encoded with a chip, and holders have a 4-digit PIN number to validate transactions rather than a signature, but credit-card machines will also read the magnetic strip cards issued by British and other banks. Some establishments – particularly supermarkets – may require other identification (such as passport) when you pay with a magnetic-strip, signature-validated card.

Where shall we go from here?

Opening hours

Commercial opening hours are increasingly flexible but these general rules will still help you. Sunday is still a day of rest, and every day the afternoon siesta is still popular (usually 12–3pm). Opening hours for tourist activities are extended in July and August.

Banks – main branches: *9am–4.30pm, Mon–Fri.*

Shops – food shops: *8am–12pm, 3–7pm; some close Mon.*

Hypermarchés – *9am–9pm, Mon–Sat.*

Tourist shops – *10am–12pm, 3–7pm; longer hours/all day July–Aug.*

Petrol stations – *8am–12pm, 3–7pm; but most have 24-hour self-service by credit card.*

Tourist offices – *10am–12pm, 2–6pm, Mon–Sat.*

Businesses – *9am–12pm, 2–6pm, Mon–Fri.*

Bars – *8am–11pm, daily.*
Churches – *9am–12pm, 2–6pm; closed to tourists during services.*
Museums – *10am–12pm, 2–6pm; longer hours/no lunch break July–Aug. National museums generally close Tue, municipal museums close Mon.*

Police

There are three main police forces in France.
Police Nationale – most commonly seen in towns and often unarmed.
Gendarmerie Nationale – deal with serious crime, also motorway law enforcement and air/sea/mountain rescue. Armed.
Compagnie Républicaine de la Sécurité (CRS) – well-armed police used for crowd control, notably serious political or social disturbances.

In addition, municipal police in most cities and many large towns deal with petty crime and traffic offences.

The police have the right to stop you and ask for identification. All French citizens must carry an identity card, so it may be wise to carry your passport with you. However, your chances of being stopped on the street for no reason are minimal.

Post offices

La Poste is an efficient and modern service. There are post offices in all major towns, with a central office and branch offices in the major cities. Post offices in smaller towns may open for limited hours (for example, mornings only).

Shops that stock postcards will also normally sell stamps (*timbres*).

Old post office in Roquebrune-Cap-Martin

Public holidays

The following dates are official holidays in France. All government buildings and banks will be closed, though not all shops, museums and tourist offices will.
1 January – New Year's Day
Easter Sunday
Easter Monday
Ascension Day – sixth Thursday after Easter
Whit Monday – second Monday after Ascension
1 May – Labour Day
8 May – VE Day
14 July – Bastille Day
15 August – Assumption Day
1 November – All Saints' Day
11 November – Remembrance Day
25 December – Christmas Day

Public transport

Tourist offices have excellent information, including timetables.

Buses – Bus services tend to operate

within *départements*, not across their boundaries. Links between major cities and towns are generally good, but services to hinterland villages may be sporadic.

Trains – there are good services along the coast, but the line runs inland between Toulon and Fréjus, north of the Massif des Maures. Using the train avoids the long queues that build up on the roads in summer, particularly between Nice and Fréjus.

Telephones

France has a modern digital telephone system (the leading company is France Telecom) and most hotels have a direct-dial system to foreign countries (though do check on prices before you call abroad, as hotels can add a huge premium to charges).

Card-operated public telephone booths are easy to find in cities and towns, and you can make direct international calls. Phone cards can be bought at tobacconists (*tabacs*) and some tourist offices. Public phones also accept credit cards.

The international code for France is 00 33. If you are calling from outside the country, do not dial the first 0 of the number.

Here are the main country codes, should you want to make an international call from France.
USA and Canada 00 1
UK 00 44
Ireland 00 353
Australia 00 61
New Zealand 00 64

Time

France operates on Central European Time, or Greenwich Mean Time plus one hour. So, if it is noon in London, it is 1pm in France. The clocks are changed for Summer Time, moving forward an hour in spring and being put back an hour in autumn.

France operates the 24-hour system when indicating time, so 10am is shown as 10:00 while 10pm is 22:00.

Tipping

It is standard practice to include a service charge in hotel, restaurant and bar prices (usually 10 per cent) – look for the phrase *service compris*. Some restaurants will add a service charge on

Card-operated phone booths are plentiful

to your final bill – look for the phrase *service non-compris*. You can leave a further gratuity if you feel the service warrants it, and also leave small amounts of change at a bar or café for the servers.

Toilets

Public toilet facilities vary in quality and cleanliness. Most cities and large towns have the modern coin-operated, self-cleaning toilets (do not allow young children to use these on their own). Smaller towns and villages usually have public toilets (often near the market place) but they may be the old 'hole in the floor' style. Carry a supply of tissue as you are not guaranteed to find any.

Police officers are approachable and helpful

Cafés and restaurants all have toilet facilities (not of a universally clean standard) but you should be a client to use them.

Tourist information

This is of a good standard. For information before you travel, contact the offices in Britain or on the Riviera:

French Government Tourist Office. *Tel: 09068 244 123* (calls at 60p per minute).

French Travel Centre, *178 Piccadilly, London, W1V 0AL*.

Comité Régional du Tourisme Riviera–Côte d'Azur (CRT), *promenade des Anglais 55, 06011 Nice. Tel: 04 93 37 78 78, www.guideriviera.com*

Once on the Riviera, you will find cities and towns have well equipped tourist information offices: look for directions to the *Office du Tourisme*. These will have information on local attractions, hotels and restaurants. Smaller communities have a *syndicat d'initiative*, usually open for limited hours in summer only, and carrying very local information. There is also an information desk at Nice-Côte d'Azur Airport open daily, 8am–10pm.

Travellers with disabilities

All new buildings must have disabled access; Cannes and Nice have wheelchair access at road crossings. However, access to older buildings can prove a problem, and hilltop villages with steep narrow cobbled lanes make access difficult.

If you have special needs, contact the CRT office – or the individual attraction, hotel or restaurant – beforehand to discuss your requirements.

The Royal Association for Disability and Rehabilitation (RADAR) in the UK publishes an annual guide called 'Holidays and Travel Abroad' and can also answer individual queries at *12, City Forum, 250 City Road, London EC1V 8AF. Tel: 020 7250 3222, www.radar.org.uk*

Bus services can help you avoid the notorious Riviera traffic jams

ACKNOWLEDGEMENTS

Thomas Cook Publishing wishes to thank PETE BENNETT for the photographs reproduced in this book, to whom the copyright in the photographs belong.

Copy-editing: JAN WILTSHIRE

Index: INDEXING SPECIALISTS (UK) LTD

Maps: PC GRAPHICS, SURREY, UK

Proof-reading: CAMBRIDGE PUBLISHING MANAGEMENT LTD and RICHARD HALL

The photographer would like to thank the tourist offices in the region for their kind assistance.